German Aircraft in Russian and Soviet Service 1914-1951

German Aircraft in Russian and Soviet Service

1914-1951

Volume I: 1914-1940

Andrei Alexandrov & Gennadi Petrov

Schiffer Military History
Atglen, PA

Translated by David Johnston

Book Design by Ian Robertson.

Library of Congress Catalog Number: 2002110224

Printed in China.
ISBN: 0-7643-1675-3

We are interested in hearing from authors with book ideas on related topics.

Published by Schiffer Publishing Ltd.
4880 Lower Valley Road
Atglen, PA 19310
Phone: (610) 593-1777
FAX: (610) 593-2002
E-mail: Schifferbk@aol.com.
Visit our web site at: www.schifferbooks.com
Please write for a free catalog.
This book may be purchased from the publisher.
Please include $3.95 postage.
Try your bookstore first.

In Europe, Schiffer books are distributed by:
Bushwood Books
6 Marksbury Avenue
Kew Gardens
Surrey TW9 4JF
England
Phone: 44 (0) 20 8392-8585
FAX: 44 (0) 20 8392-9876
E-mail: Bushwd@aol.com.
Free postage in the UK. Europe: air mail at cost.
Try your bookstore first.

FOREWORD

The First World War was the last in which troops of Imperial Russia took part. Prior to the end of hostilities, revolution broke out in St. Petersburg and quickly spread to all parts of the Russian Empire from the Baltic to the Pacific. Influenced by these events, the Eastern Front collapsed.

The civil war in Russia resulted in a new state, the Union of Soviet Socialist Republics, which lasted more than seventy years until the events of the 1990s brought about the collapse of the USSR.

The first half of the Twentieth Century saw the transformation of Russia from an absolute monarchy to fateful totalitarianism. One thing remained unchanged, however, "fear of Germany."

Paradoxically, relations between the two states continuously alternated between economic relationships and military confrontations.

Curiously, none of the other totalitarian states which developed in the 1930s found any common basis for closer relations with the USSR. Dogmatic principles which developed in their policies prevented this.

Idealistic conformity gained the upper hand over realistic estimation. This may have saved the world from an even greater catastrophe, however, it led the people of the USSR and Germany into a great tragedy.

Relations in the field of aviation were in one way contrary, and in another in keeping with, general Soviet and German policies. Under the limitations of this situation German aviation developed into a part of Soviet aviation.

Stated succinctly, this explains the importance which is credited to the presence of German aircraft in the Soviet Union.

Testing of these aircraft resulted in major gains in aviation knowledge in both countries. Researching this theme reveals many gaps, however. Revolution, war, and other tumultuous events have destroyed much evidence of this history. Then there is the time factor.

On the other hand, propaganda influences prevented the publicizing of certain events, and often led to historical fabrications. Politics also played a role.

Many technical details have remained classified to the present day and are accessible to only a few persons. In addition, certain information has been intentionally falsified. Two world wars have given research into this theme a strongly "hostile image."

The tragedy of the "Great Patriotic War" understandably caused interest in German technology to wane. As well, the memories of those who were there have waned with the passage of time. Terminology presented additional difficulties. German aircraft were "foreign aircraft," which received different designations. Thus, in some cases the German designation, which provided clues as to airframe, power plant, etc., could not be confirmed. Much important information was lost as a result. One could provide many other reasons for the difficulty of researching this complexity of themes. One of the greatest problems, however, was the inaccessibility of archives and data collections. Numerous works have been written (in the USSR) on the activities of German aircraft on the Eastern Front, many of them by participants in the air war, but they are also official military histories.

Unfortunately, these publications provide little useful information. Indeed, in the past forty years a trend has become obvious to speak, in very general terms, of initial losses and certain problems in the later stages of the war. Ultimately, however, Soviet aviation was given absolute priority.

Countless illustrations in books, some portraying realistic scenes, some imaginary ones, had one theme: the success and heroism of the Soviet aviator.

The German air force was portrayed in rather darker shades, which inevitably led to a false estimation. Curiously, in the past ten years books have appeared in the same one-sided style but from the other point of view, placing the role of constant failure on the Soviet air force.

Neither approach is objective. The absence of western literature on this theme and the inability to hear the opinions of western historians on this topic make a closer examination of the events on the Eastern Front impossible.

Taking all factors into consideration, it is unlikely that a more accurate depiction will be possible in the near future, especially since many western publications have a fragmentary character, and therefore must be seen as historic in nature.

Fifty years of cooperation between the USSR and Germany in the field of aviation is at best a tile in the mosaic of history. But it should not be forgotten that hundreds, indeed thousands of people were involved in the activity and were influenced by it to some degree.

It is our intention to tackle all areas of detail in future publications. There is hope that changes in the former Soviet camp will one day permit a complete examination of this theme.

The material compiled here may undoubtedly be classified as "significant." It is the result of lengthy and intensive research. Information which has reached us recently gives cause for hope that future research may lead to further successes. The most important basis for this work, however, is the steadily growing interest in this half-forgotten subject.

I would be pleased if interested readers would correct errors and provide additional information for future publications. I feel a deep obligation to express my sincere thanks to those people who gave us invaluable assistance. In particular I would like to thank Natalia Vinevskaya and Nikolaevna Aleksandrova, who worked on the English and Russian editions of this book, and Alexander Smirnov, who translated the book into German and thus made a major contribution to the realization of this project.

To Andrey Khrapov and Oleg Zatzepin for their assistance in solving technical problems. And to Victor Kulikov, whose information illuminated a large part of the First World War.

Mikhail Maslov and Konstantin Kosminkov kindly made available their rare material. We wish to thank Vladimir Klimov, Valery Bulba, Dmitry Grinjuk and Vadim Zaitzev, who also made valuable contributions. We would also like to express special thanks to Harry Woodman, Nigel Eastaway, Malcolm Passingham, and Manfred Franzke, without whose help this project would not have been possible.

The authors sincerely hope that you, the reader, will enjoy this book.

Andrei Alexandrov
Gennadi Petrov
St. Petersburg
February 1997

Advertisement by the Albatros Werke, published in the Russian magazine *Bulletin of Aeronautics* in 1912. The ad described Albatros as a supplier of aircraft to the German *Fliegertruppe* and foreign armies.
Albatros Antoinette type monoplane (single- and two-seat racing machine) with 65 HP Antoinette Argus, or 100 HP Gnome engines.
Albatros biplane, Farman or Sommer type with 50 HP and 100 HP Gnome or 65 HP Renault and Austro-Daimler engines.
Albatros aircraft are also used by the Russian pilots A. Grunberg, Lindpaintner, Brunnhuber, Wintzirs, Kenig, Laitch, and the Swiss pilot Rupp.

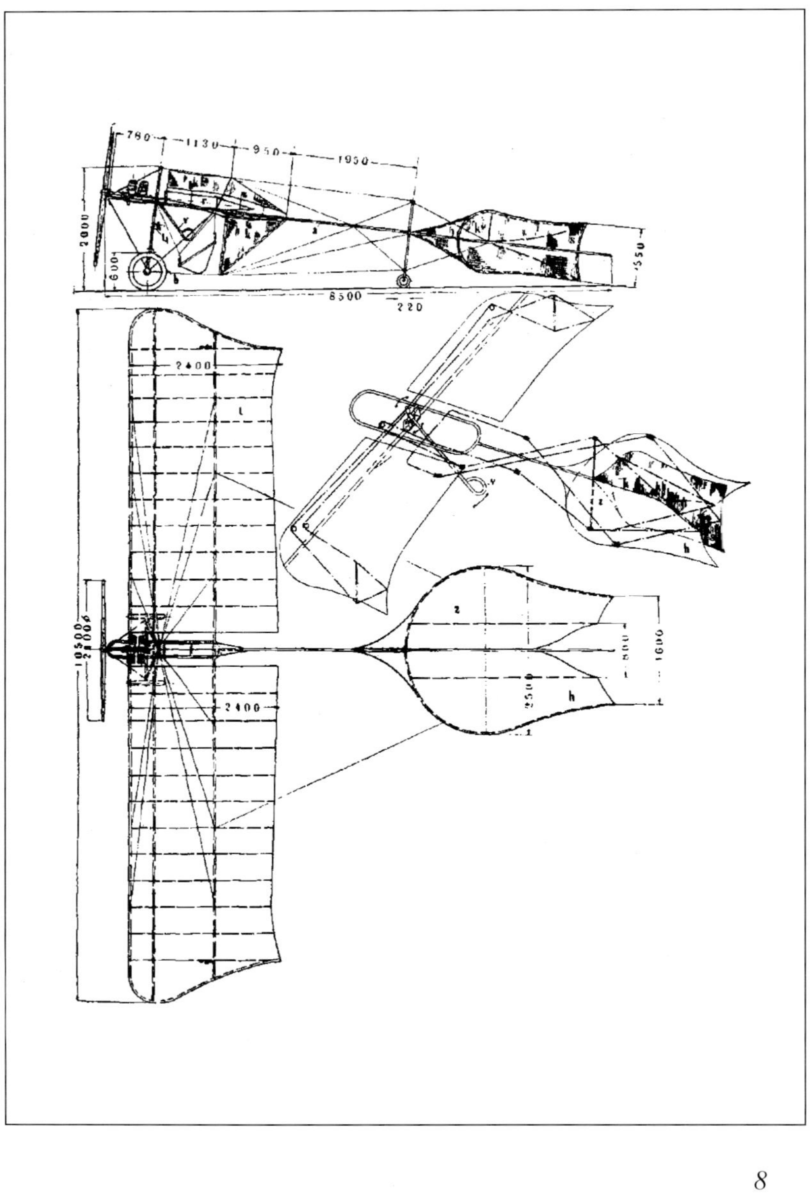

Three-view drawing of a Grade Monoplane powered by a 40 HP Grade engine. The plan appeared in *Vestnik Vozdushoplavania* in 1911.

1911-1914

Practical aviation began in the time of the Wright Brothers, who spread the beginnings of aviation over the entire world. Aviation enthusiasts in many nations built flying machines and took to the air. The risks were great. At the same time, far-sighted businessmen recognized the potential of this budding field of technology.

Nations with a high degree of economical, intellectual and technical potential were, of course, the first to produce aircraft and train pilots. The secret of aircraft design soon became common knowledge. The development process took on international dimensions. All of Europe, including Germany and Russia, was seized by aviation fever.

The first German aircraft arrived in Russia between 1909 and 1911. From that time on, German technicians were an almost permanent fixture in Russia.

Historical records indicate that the first aircraft was a Grade Monoplane, which arrived in Russia in 1909. Another machine of this type was displayed at an exhibition in St. Petersburg in 1911, along with a two-seat Harlan powered by a 65 H.P. engine.

The first, albeit limited, military use of aircraft took place in 1912. As the aircraft's potential as a weapon was demonstrated, the military began showing a greater interest. In Russia, the first comparison and test flights of various types, including foreign designs, took place in 1912.

One of the aircraft which made an impression in the competition was the Spider, a design by the recently founded Fokker Company. It took fourth place. At that time Fokker was based in Berlin-Johannisthal.

Two aircraft from the Deutschen Flugzeugwerke Leipzig also took part in the competition. One aircraft was a biplane powered by a 100-H.P. Argus engine, the other was a monoplane equipped with a 120-H.P. Daimler engine with frontal radiator. Both aircraft performed bravely but neither was selected for purchase.

The first known Russian purchase of a German-built aircraft occurred in 1912. It was a Farman powered by a Gnome engine and built under licence by Albatros. The aircraft was destined for a flying school in Gatchina near Petersburg. At about the same time two Taube aircraft designed by the Austrian engineer Igor Etrich arrived in Russia. One of these machines was flown by pilots Jankovski and Lerkhe.

The Taube was one of the most widely-used aircraft of its day. Most important German aircraft manufacturers, including Rumpler, Albatros and DFW, built the Taube under license.

Several other German aircraft visited Russia prior to 1914, including machines built by LVG, Rumpler and Albatros. There are clues to a proposed purchase of an Albatros powered by a 60-H.P. Mercedes engine, however negotiations were unsuccessful.

One interesting story concerns a biplane built by the German designer Fitinghoff which appeared in Petersburg in 1912. The aircraft had gigantic wheels as tall as a man and therefore received the nickname "Kolesnitza Il'ya Ilias" (The Prophet Elias' Wagon). The aircraft was not flown because of structural problems.

From this account it is obvious that German aircraft did not play a major role in Russian aviation prior to the First World War. The trend was more toward France, which was an ally of Russia.

Russia's aviation industry developed quickly, with 157 aircraft projects being realized between 1909 and 1913. Of these, 105 were flown successfully. The most promising designs originated from Igor Sikorsky. His four-engined Ilya Murometz became world-famous. The aircraft was the first multi-engine bomber to enter service anywhere.

By 1913 production of aircraft had reached 23 per month, however the Russian industry's ability to support its products did not match its developmental capacity. This became painfully apparent when the first German aircraft were met in combat.

Appendix

Vestnik Vozdukhoplavania
(Air Fleet Report No. 5 / 1912)

Statistics of fatal aviation accidents to 1 January 1912:

	Number of pilots	Accidents	%
Germany	133	13	9.77
Russia	103	4	3.88

Vestnik Vozdukhoplavania
(Air Fleet Report No. 6-7 / 1912)

On 3 March pilots Kamensky and Slavorossov conducted three flights in an Etrich Taube at the Mokotovskoye airfield.

Vestnik Vozdukhoplavania
(Air Fleet Report No. 7-8 / 1912)

The following number of pilot licenses was issued by 1 January 1911:

Germany	46
Russia	7

Vestnik Vozdukhoplavania
(Air Fleet Report No. 11 / 1912)

On 21 August a competition for militarily suitable aircraft, organized by the military department, began at the Korpusnoy airfield (near Petersburg).

Participants are:

I.I. Sikorsky with a biplane of his own design.
G.V. Yanovsky in the Sikorsky aircraft.
Butmi de Katzman in a Duks monoplane.
G.V. Alechovich in a Gakkel design.

Taking part outside the competition were V.M. Abramovich in a Wright aircraft and Fokker in a machine of his own design.

Vestnik Vozdukhoplavania
(Air Fleet Report No. 12 / 1912)

Although the military competition at the Korpusnoy airfield, Petersburg is soon to end, it is proceeding extremely slowly. Reasons are the poor weather conditions and the poor serviceability of the aircraft. None of the aircraft has met the conditions of the competition. Two aircraft (a monoplane and a biplane) from the Mars Company came from Germany. Pilot Lieutenant Bier, a participant in the Berlin-Vienna flight, easily met all the conditions of the competition in a Mars monoplane in two days.

Vestnik Vozdukhoplavania
(Air Fleet Report No. 14 / 1912)

The military competition for aircraft, which began on 20 August, has ended. The aircraft of the German participants: Abramovich in the Wright, Fokker and two Mars, monoplane and biplane. All flew outside the competition.

Vestnik Vozdukhoplavania
(Air Fleet Report No. 14 / 1912)

Performance comparison between the Fokker monoplane and the victorious Sikorsky biplane during the competition for military aircraft:

	Fokker	Sikorsky
Maximum speed (km/h)	97	113.3
Climb to 500 m (min.)	8.7	6.4
Takeoff distance (m)	107.3	120
Landing distance (m)	52.3	36
Minimum speed (km/h)	74.4	76.5
Time to partially dismantle (min.)	6.2	7.1
Engine output (H.P.)	92	92
Empty weight (kg)	530	590
Time to completely dismantle (min.)	41	18.2

In terms of view from the cockpit and servicing, the aircraft were judged to be equal. The German aircraft was assessed better in terms of landing in poor field conditions and gunnery potential.

Vestnik Vozdukhoplavania
(Air Fleet Report No. 14 / 1912)

The aviatrix L.A. Galanchikova is now in Johannisthal, where she has already made more than 30 successful flights in a Fokker monoplane.

The Period from 1914-1917

The First World War began on 1 August 1914. Russia had completed mobilizing its forces at the end of July. Russian military aviation was divided into 39 small detachments and six aviation companies, which were attached to the balloon depots. The total number of aircraft on strength was 244.

At the outset of the war Germany found herself in a worse strategic position. Russia had just one, albeit extremely long, front, while from the outset Germany was forced to fight on two fronts. As a result of this situation Russia initially enjoyed numerical superiority in the air, however, no visible results were achieved, as its aircraft lacked any offensive or defensive armament. Meetings between opposing machines in the air were peaceful, but soon opposing crews began trying to shoot down their opposite numbers with pistols and rifles. Efforts were even made to bring down opposing aircraft with hand grenades, or a hook attached to a long wire. The latter method was used by the Russian pilot A.A. Kozakov.

Not surprisingly, none of these methods was effective, and some pilots resulted to more desperate measures. On 9 March 1915 Kozakov rammed a German Albatros after his hook method proved unsuccessful. He was the first pilot on the Eastern Front to ram an enemy machine and survive.

The first actual ramming attack was made by Staff Captain P.N. Nesterov on 28 August 1914. The Morane and the German Albatros both crashed, killing Nesterov and the crew of the German machine (Rosenthal and observer).

Aerial bombing was also in its infancy, and the first Russian bombing unit was not formed until four months after the outbreak of war. The unit was titled *Eskadra Vozdushnykh Korabley* and was equipped with Sikorsky Ilya Murometz aircraft.

A similar German unit called *Brieftaubenabteilung Ostende* (Ostend Carrier Pigeon Battalion) was formed in September 1914, and was transferred to the Eastern Front in the spring of 1915. The unit's mission was to conduct offensive air operations in support of the *XI. Armee* in Galicia.

In the first months of the war the primary role of aviation was reconnaissance and artillery spotting. German reconnaissance aircraft played a decisive role in the fighting in East Prussia in August 1914. Information brought back by pilots of the *43.* and *14. Fliegerabteilung* was instrumental in the destruction of Samsonov's 11th Army.

Both sides suffered heavy losses. Some sources report 146 Russian aircraft lost by the end of 1914. The detachments assigned to the 3rd, 5th, 8th, and 9th Armies on the southwestern front saw their original complement of 99 aircraft reduced to just 8 machines. These losses were caused by technical deficiencies, inexperienced pilots, and of course, enemy action.

The poor state of the Russian aviation industry meant that little could be done to change this state of affairs. The favorable position enjoyed by Russian aviation at the outset deteriorated as the war went on. Aircraft production rates climbed slowly. The engine production situation was especially critical. While it may be said that production of fabric-covered airframes was organized to some degree, the same never applied to the production of aero-engines.

Russia was forced to purchase equipment from France and England, and these contacts were maintained even after the war. The Russian government purchased approximately 1,800 aircraft and 4,000 engines from allied nations. Russian industry produced just 1,511 engines, compared to the 40,449 built by the German aviation industry.

The situation in the air deteriorated rapidly when the first Fokker E-type monoplanes appeared on the Eastern Front. These machines were armed with a machine-gun which fired through the propeller arc. From that point on the air war entered a new phase. New tactics led to a reorganization of Russian air units.

The second half of 1916 saw the formation of 12 reorganized fighter detachments and aviation groups, each consisting of four to six small detachments. The increased strength of the new units made it possible for them to again undertake large-scale operations.

At approximately the same time the Germans introduced the so-called *"Jastas"* (*Jagdstaffeln*, or fighter squadrons). The number of German fighter aces eventually reached the proud figure of 366, with Manfred Baron von Richthofen leading the way with 80 victories.

Russian results were less spectacular. Twenty-six Russian aces destroyed 188 enemy aircraft. The leading Russian fighter ace was A.A. Kozakov with 17 aerial victories.

The air war over the Eastern Front was intensive, and at times bitter, however, the German forces had a relatively easy time of it. This was largely due to the poor serviceability rates of the Russian air forces caused by technical problems. This situation even allowed the Germans to reduce the number of aircraft assigned to the Eastern Front.

The Russian air forces reached their maximum strength around mid-1917, with 135 wings. The total number of aircraft was 1,031, of which 581 were serviceable.

The monthly loss rate, based on the requisition lists from the period 1 January 1917 to 1 July 1918, was 17% for bombers, 37% for reconnaissance aircraft, and 50% for fighters.

Figures published after the war place German losses between 1914 and 1918 at 2,128 aircraft written off, 5,136 damaged, and approximately 1,000 which fell into enemy hands. Of the latter, approximately 120-150 machines were captured by the Russians. They were German- and Austrian-built machines operated by German, Austrian, and Turkish units.

On 25 September 1917, for example, a Turkish aircraft was forced down on Russian soil. It was an Albatros Type 1917 biplane powered by a Daimler Benz engine and armed with Hotchkiss and Maxim machine-guns. The aircraft's equipment included a radio, camera, compass, and bombs. The machine-guns fired tracing ammunition, which allowed the gunner to correct his aim.

The aircraft's Turkish pilot, Vedigi Fegan, stated that his unit had six more aircraft of the same type. The cost of the aircraft was 2,500 Turkish Lira, or approximately 21,500 Rubles, which was equivalent to the cost of two Grigorovich M-5 flying boats.

Damaged or unserviceable aircraft were repaired in military front-line repair facilities or by unit mechanics. If the damage was too great, the aircraft were returned to the manufacturers, and they were repaired and returned to the units. Some units operated captured equipment exclusively. As early as 1914 the XVIII Air Corps was equipped solely with captured German aircraft, and operated them until the end of 1916. Aircraft known to have been operated by the unit were: Albatros No. 128, 187, 252, 289, 373, and 384, and a single Rumpler. Albatros 128 and 252 were written off in November 1915. At the beginning of 1916 these aircraft were replaced by an Aviatik B II powered by a 150-HP Daimler motor. It was flown until January 1917.

Captured aircraft were also used by the XXIII Air Corps. One such machine was Albatros No. 389. Following its capture it was assigned to an aviation detachment. On 13 April 1915 pilot Poruchik Georgy Boreish and observer Paruchik Leontiev took off on a reconnaissance flight. They failed to return. It was assumed that they had been captured.

The majority of the captured enemy aircraft were two-seat reconnaissance aircraft. Fighters and twin-engined bombers were the exception.

The first captured aircraft was an Albatros three-bay biplane. Approximately ten such machines were flown in Russian service. They were equipped with a variety of power plants, such as Mercedes, Benz, Argus, and Austro Daimler producing 80 to 100 HP. It should be noted that the main identifying feature of captured aircraft was engine output, consequently the precise Albatros or Rumpler variant can only be guessed at. Basically, one can assume the following types:

Albatros with 120-200 HP engines.
Rumpler with Mercedes and Opel engines (200-220 HP)
LVG with Benz and Mercedes engines (200-220 HP)
The most frequently captured variants were the Albatros B II, C I, C III, C V, C VII, C X, and C XII reconnaissance machines.
Rumpler B I, C I, C IV, C V.
LVG C V, C VI.
Halberstadt C V.
Most Halberstadt were fighters powered by 120-160 HP Argus engines.
Rolands with monocoque fuselages and Fokkers with Oberursel rotary engines producing approximately 100 HP.
Also Halberstadt D Ia, D II, D III, and D IV.
LVG D II and Fokker E.
Russian naval aviation also employed captured German aircraft, such as Hansa-Brandenburg W-12, W-25, W-32, GW, and NW seaplanes.
Sablatnig SF-5 and Friedrichshafen FF49c.

Captured aircraft served with the Russian air forces throughout the First World War and into the early 1920s. During their service lives they were overhauled, and in some cases fitted with new equipment and armament.

At the urging of a Russian pilot, in 1916 an Albatros was fitted with a Colt machine-gun. The experiment proved extremely successful, and on 16 February 1916 was officially authorized by the army. As a result of this, orders were issued for the arming of Russian aircraft prior to the spring offensive. It was hoped that this would improve the operational capabilities of the Russian air forces, especially as machine-guns were in wide use in German aircraft and were being installed on the production line.

It is also noteworthy that the Russian aircraft industry copied a number of German aircraft designs. Although the development of domestic types continued, copies of successful enemy designs were used with success. This enabled the manufacturers to save time and money.

One company which limited production to copies of German types was V.A. Lebedev of St. Petersburg. This type of activity began in 1915 when an Albatros (150 HP) built in 1914 (probably a B II) was sent to the company. It became the basis for a whole family of aircraft under the name Lebied XI (company designation Typ1 A-1 Biplane). These machines differed from the original in wingspan and engine output. As many as six different types of spars were used, and there were two- and three-bay types. Wingspan varied from 13 to 14.5 meters, and wing area between 39 and 43.6 square meters. The aircraft were powered by captured German power plants that were overhauled in Russian workshops. The most common engines were Mercedes (100 to 150 HP), Benz (120, 140, and 150 HP), and Maybach (160 HP).

Lebied XIs were built in 1915 and 1916, and production totaled about 10 aircraft. Subsequent aircraft were powered by a Salmson air-cooled engine (159 HP). This was the first step to a further design, the Lebied XII. The Salmson engine was the only power plant built in quantity in Russia, and was a natural choice to power the aircraft.

Work on the prototype began in mid-1915, and in December the aircraft took to the air powered by a 130 HP Salmson. The test report states that on 28 December 1915 military pilot Poruchik Sleptzov took to the air in the Lebied XII serial number 325 (Salmson engine No. 611, 130 HP). Two flights were made, each lasting 15 minutes. Sleptzov complained about several teething problems, but admitted that the aircraft's handling qualities were superior to the German Albatros. He also found that the type was faster and had less engine vibration. On 19 June 1915 the company received a contract to build 225 machines.

Series production began in August 1916 and lasted two years. Trials were also carried out with a version equipped with a more powerful Salmson engine (140 HP). Production of the Lebied XII continued under the Soviets until 1924. A total of 216 aircraft were laid down, of which 192 were completed, most with the 150 HP Salmson engine.

In service the aircraft proved less than successful, however. It was difficult to handle in the air, and recovering from a dive was impossible. As well, the engine had a tendency to catch fire. By 1917 the type was obsolescent, however, it continued to be used because of the precarious aircraft situation.

In 1917 Lebedev produced several machines with other modifications. These included several three-bay Albatros powered by a variety of engines, including Sanbim, Duflon, Konstantionovich M 101, and Fiat types.

Two further types based on German designs, the Lebied XIII and Lebied XXIV, appeared in 1917. The former was a development of the earlier aircraft with a 230 HP Fiat engine. Three hundred examples of this type were built. The latter type was supposed to be powered by a 230 HP Fiat or 200 HP Hispano engine. Initial plans called for 200 machines to be built, but in the end the type did not enter production. After the October Revolution the Allies halted deliveries of aviation technology and engines.

Other types were developed or repaired in the period 1915-1916. These included three-bay Albatros with 100-120 HP Austro-Daimler engines, Albatros with Isotta Frascati (150-170 HP), Mercedes (160 HP), and Benz (150 HP) engines, LVG C II with the designation Lebied IX, Rumpler and Aviatik types with various power plants, and Fokkers with Gnome Rhone engines. Lebied aircraft were also built by other Russian aircraft manufacturers.

The Lebedev company also tried copying seaplanes. One of these was the Lebied Morskoi LM-1 powered by a Sanbim engine (150 HP) built in 1916. It was a three-bay biplane with three floats (two main and one tail float). Although it was originally powered by a Renault engine (220 HP), the LM-1 was nothing more than a floatplane version of the standard Lebied landplane.

By 1917 the navy desperately needed an aircraft with rearward-firing machine-guns for defense against enemy fighter attack. Lebedev proposed a copy of the German Albatros seaplane, which in pilot circles had the nickname "Beetle." This requirement was unrealistic, however, as Russia had no inline engine in the 200 HP class.

On 14 June 1917 the navy ordered 175 machines, which were to be built in the factory in Taganrog, on the Sea of Azov. Only two machines were completed, however, in December 1917, and these were powered by a 200 HP Hispano engine.

The Anadva VH, a Russian design by V.N. Hioni which appeared in the summer of 1917, used original Albatros floats. Another Russian company that based its designs on a German type was A.D. Anatra in Odessa. It produced two-seat reconnaissance biplanes with two struts beneath each wing. The designs incorporated German experience, however, they were not direct copies of German types. The Anatra aircraft possessed excellent performance.

On the whole, the copying of enemy aircraft and the repairing of captured machines demonstrated the weakness of the entire Russian aircraft industry. The art of copying proved useful, however, as it did result in the acquisition of some technology. The knowledge gained in this way was used in later developments.

Appendix

Vestnik Vozdushnogo Flota
Report by the Air Fleet No. 2 1918

Information on shot-down enemy aircraft in the period from September 1916 to September 1917.

1916

On September 10 aircraft were shot down by 14 balloon companies with rifle and machine-gun fire. The aircraft had struck the cables.

On 23 November the 2nd Observer Station of the 17th Balloon Company shot down an aircraft with rifle and machine-gun fire. Pilot and observer were captured. The aircraft was largely undamaged.

On 11 March the 37th Balloon Corps shot down an aircraft. The crew were taken prisoner.

On 13 March a balloon of the 9th Balloon Section set an aircraft on fire. The aircraft came under machine-gun fire from the unit and rifle fire from other soldiers. It crashed soon afterwards near the town of Novosiolki, resulting in major damage to the right wing. The seriously injured pilot and observer were captured.

On 14 June an enemy aircraft used an explosive device to bring down a balloon of the 25th Army Balloon Section. Machine-gun and rifle fire was directed at the machine, which glided in the direction of its own territory and was reported to have come down near an enemy barbed wire obstacle.

On 17 June the 18th Army Balloon Section shot down an aircraft with machine-gun and rifle fire as it was attacking one of our balloons. The aircraft crashed near the village of Mshany. One rocket launcher, two rockets, and a machine-gun belt with ammunition were captured.

On 23 June the 9th Corps Balloon Section shot down an aircraft after it had set a balloon on fire. The shock wave from the exploding hydrogen caused the machine to go out of control and crash approximately 150 paces from the burning balloon. Both pilots were found dead and showed evidence of bullet wounds.

On 1 June the 45th Corps Balloon Section shot down an aircraft with machine-gun fire after it had set a balloon on fire. According to the battalion the machine came down in no man's land between our trenches and those of the 3rd Romanian Corps.

On 25 July a German aircraft was shot down by machine-gun and rifle fire from the 4th Army Balloon Section after it attacked the balloon unit. The pilot was killed. The aircraft, with functional engine, instruments, and machine-gun, was handed over to the 4th Army Aviation Battalion.

On 26 July a second enemy aircraft was shot down while attacking a balloon during the ascent phase. Parts of the aircraft were handed over to the 71st Infantry Division. The balloon was undamaged.

At 1130 hours on 25 August, the 1st Army Balloon Section shot down an aircraft. The observer Gubarev reported that the aircraft came down between the lines near the village of Galichany.

At 1345 hours on 25 August, the 1st Army Balloon Section shot down its second aircraft, which was also attacking a balloon. The aircraft crashed near Bevestechko. The pilots were taken prisoner.

At 1050 hours on 25 August the 20th Army Balloon Section shot down an aircraft, which came down between the lines.

At 1100 hours on 27 August an aircraft attacked a balloon of the 10th Army Balloon Section and was shot down by cannon, machine-gun, and rifle fire. The aircraft was destroyed, and the pilot killed. The balloon was not damaged.

On 16 September the 11th Army Balloon Section shot down an aircraft with machine-gun fire after it attempted to attack the balloon. The balloon was not damaged. The aircraft was set on fire by its crew before they were taken prisoner.

Above: Wooden altar in front of a German aircraft in memory of the victims of the war. Above Right: Aviatik B II of the 5th Austrian Air Division. While on a reconnaissance flight on 5 January 1916 the aircraft suffered engine failure and made a forced landing. The aircraft was subsequently employed by the Russian 18th Corps' Aviation Division until January-February 1917.

Captured Rumpler C I with the code C429 on the vertical fin. Evidence of fire is visible on the wings and port side of the fuselage.

Partially disassembled Roland D II following capture by Russian forces. The photo was taken in the Ukraine in 1917.

Visible behind this Breguet XIV are several disassembled LVGs. The Breguet fell into Russian hands on the southern front during the civil war, along with its French pilot Lacombe (in 1919 or 1920).

Junkers CL 1 with wings and vertical tail removed. It is believed that two of these aircraft fell into Russian hands on the southern front, however, they were not taken into the Russian inventory. The aircraft's code reads 1803 or 803/18.

An interesting photo of two Albatros C VIIs undergoing repair work. Although the personnel are clearly German, the photo was discovered in a Russian album entitled "Russian Aviation Activities in the Riga Area."

This Roland D II was shot down by pilot Sveshnikov in 1917. The aircraft's port undercarriage was damaged in the ensuing forced landing.

The same aircraft from a different angle.

A welcome addition; a captured Austrian Aviatik B III.

Top and right: This Roland D II was captured in the spring of 1917. Here Russian fighter pilots inspect the machine closely.

A Lebied XII of the 6th Army Aviation Unit Petrograd. The photo was probably taken in 1916.

LVG C V of a Russian air unit.

AEG. C IV after a crash-landing. The trailing edge of the aileron is interesting. Note the unusual shape of the Soviet star beneath the wing. The points of the star are curved rather than straight, resulting in a shape which more closely resembles a flower than a star.

Roland D II in Soviet service in 1920-21. The significance of the heroic motif around the Soviet star is not known. The unusual windscreen was probably the result of a modification.

Albatros B I. This photo was probably taken during the winter of 1914-15.

The well-known Russian aviator Artzeulov (second from left) next to an Albatros. Artzeulov was one of the first Russian pilots, and later achieved many firsts in Soviet aviation.

Group photo of Russian pilots in front of an Albatros three-bay biplane. Unfortunately, the names of the pilots are not known.

While the officers pose for another photograph, a mechanic turns the large propeller of an Albatros B II.

Servicing an Albatros B II.

This Albatros B II was also a captured aircraft that entered service with the Russian armed forces. Note the Russian insignia on the wings.

The Period from 1917-1921

The February Revolution of 1917 had little effect on the Russian position. Military operations continued in the Eastern and Caucasus Fronts and the country remained an ally of Great Britain and France. The state remained a functioning mechanism. Territorially, it suffered little, apart from the territories lost to the Germans. Russia was vital to the Allied cause as never before. After the Bolshevik Revolution of October 1917, however, the situation changed dramatically.

Several radical political parties promised peace and freedom, however they were unable to fulfill these promises and their proclamations merely reflected the pitiless struggle taking place for mastery of the suffering nation. The collapse of Imperial Russia accelerated, plunging the land into political and economic chaos. The military front collapsed and desertion became epidemic.

By the spring of 1918 there was no unified power in the state. Germany's policies toward its former enemy followed two paths. The first was to separate Russia from its former allies as quickly as possible, allowing it co concentrate forces in the west for the decisive struggle there. To achieve this aim, Germany secretly and officially gave support to political forces, including the Bolsheviks, in Russia and the Ukraine.

On the other side Germany could not resist the urge for territorial aggrandizement and, following the collapse of the Eastern Front, occupied the Baltic States, Byelorussia, elements of the Ukraine, and the Crimea. The situation of aviation, now under control of the Bolsheviks, was dramatic in every respect.

Only 33 of the 135 former Russian air units came under Soviet control in 1918. They operated approximately 300 aircraft, most of which were obsolescent. The machines were in constant need of repair, which proved difficult under the strained conditions of civil war. The operation staff's situation was equally difficult. Former pilots of the Czar's army took the opportunity to defect and flew their aircraft to the enemy's of the Soviet powers.

In May 1919 Victor Khodorovich, former commander of the 8th Aviation Battalion, was sent to the Soviet-Hungarian Republic in his 220-H.P. LVG. The flight, which followed the route Vinnitsa—Budapest—Vinnitsa, was successful.

Khodorovich later became head of the Kiever flying school, however he was accused of being lukewarm in his support for the struggle of the proletariat and of certain vanities, such as wearing silver suspenders with black eagles. In 1918 Khodorovich flew his mechanic and his wife to territory held by the Deniken Army.

The era of flights to Hungary ended with the flight by pilot Anders in his LVG C V carrying a passenger, the Swiss communist Platen. The aircraft crash-landed in Romania and the pair were arrested. Aside from the episode involving Khodorovich, the flights to Hungary are interesting in that they were carried out exclusively with German-made aircraft. It appears that they were thoroughly reliable machines which could be trusted for such political missions.

German aircraft were used in Soviet aviation's military training schools through the entire period to 1922. Everything possible was extracted from the aircraft. They were flown until wear reached the point where they were no longer capable of taking to the air. The Soviets also attempted to assemble aircraft from components from crashed machines.

Following the withdrawal of English forces from Arkhangelsk, units of the Red Army discovered engines which had reached the end of their service lives and had been left behind by the English. The engines were subsequently repaired and placed back in service.

Inadequate servicing led to a large number of accidents. In those days obituaries of pilots and mechanics filled the pages of aviation magazines. The following accidents occurred between 23 April 1918 and 20 April 1920:

A pilot of the 2nd Kostroma Aviation Battalion crashed his Albatros, which was powered by a Fiat engine, from a height of 80 meters and was killed.

Three further accidents involved an Albatros and two LVGs. Two Albatros were damaged in forced landings and three Hansa Brandenburgs were destroyed on airfields.

The accident statistics from this period contain 60 serious accidents with fatal casualties and 307 minor accidents. The precise number of German aircraft involved is not known.

The total number of aircraft lost in the period was 422. Two of these were lost in aerial combat, 23 fell into enemy hands or were reported missing. A total of 32 aircraft were flown to the enemy by deserting pilots.

These figures give some idea of the activities of the Soviet air command. A pilot of the 13th Aviation Battalion with the name of Choralko was included in this sad list when his Nieuport shed its wings in flight. It was reported that he was a captured German pilot who had been flying since 1912. From 1919 he was active as a mechanic with the Kiever flying school and later served as a flight instructor in Kiev and Moscow.

Accidents were regular occurrences and were usually due to mechanical causes. In December 1929 an "Albatros" (C X or C XII) was lost during a flight from the Evlach air force base into the mountains. The aircraft shed its wings and all aboard were killed.

But German aircraft also figured prominently in other areas. Many of the significant events of early Soviet aviation involved German machines.

In may 1921 pilot N.V. Vasiliev flew an LVG C V from Odessa to Kharkov in a flight which lasted 5 hours and 30 minutes.

On 14 January of the same year, B.K. Velling, a pilot with a unit on the Turkestan Front, and his observer flew an LVG C V from Poltoratzk to Termez and back, covering a total distance of 2450 km. The aircraft was in the air for 22 hours and 45 minutes and flew at an altitude of 600 meters. During the civil war the LVG earned a reputation every bit as good as that of the Albatros during the First World War. The latter was well known from its length of service, but admittedly the Albatros possessed a number of shortcomings. The gap it left behind was filled by LVGs.

In addition to the Red Army, German types also served other governments which formed in lands formerly part of Imperial Russia. The Crimean Republic was formed in May 1918. When the new republic failed to create an aviation system, Germany provided aircraft and equipment. Russian pilots remained in the Crimea to keep an eye on the Germans. The German detachments were stationed in Simferopol and later Sevastopol. The Russian observers were impressed by the orderly ground organization and extraordinary discipline in the air.

German units were also stationed in the areas of the Ukraine occupied in 1918. The Ukrainian state was organized later that year. On 16 January 1919 the government of Soviet Russia declared war.

S.V. Petlura was placed in charge of the Ukrainian armed forces in February. His army included two aviation divisions, divided into headquarters, flying schools and aviation maintenance facilities. All equipment was German. In 1919 the Ukrainian government purchased about 30 aircraft, including LVGs, a Gotha and an Austrian Lohner. The LVGs cost 45,000 marks apiece.

The Ukrainian air units moved from place to place together with the Petlura Army. The flying schools were also moved constantly. German pilots visited Petlura's army, helping deliver the new Ukrainian currency which had been printed in Germany. Flights between Berlin and the Ukraine were carried out with LVGs, Rumplers, Sablatnigs and twin-engined AEG and Friedrichshafen aircraft of the Deutsche Luftreederei, all of which had been modified for civilian use.

It is not known which types were flown in the Ukraine itself, but the company and its pilots logged a total of 32000 kilometers.

The same company also made winter relief flights to Soviet Russia, delivering medicines to prisoners of war in the winter of 1920.

The Deutsche Luftreederei was founded in 1917. Passenger, freight and mail service began on 5 February 1919. By November 1920 the company had logged one million kilometers flown. Despite the civil war, the activities of this company did not go unnoticed by the Soviets. Moscow displayed a keen interest in the events taking place in Germany, its former enemy. It was of course too soon for rapprochement, but the mass media did display a certain sympathy for Germany.

Typical was the headline "Vandalism", which headed an article on the scrapping of 22,000 engines and 14,000 aircraft in Germany. Other articles featured interviews with pilots who flew the Berlin to Moscow route in which they described the state of aviation in Germany. It was learned that aviation was restricted to cultural purposes, that military aviation had been forbidden, that strict Allied controls had reduced civilian aviation to a low level, and that Allied inspectors—mainly French—were hampering the development of German aviation.

The interviews with the pilots also dealt with technical developments. It was at this time that the name Junkers first appeared in the press. Soon his aircraft would write a new page in the history of aviation in the USSR.

Appendix

Vestnik Vozdushnogo Flota
Air Fleet Report No. 2 dated 1918

Moscow, July 1918

We are now completely isolated and cut off from Western Europe. This situation has gone on for 10 months already and the last information on the state of the Allied and German air forces dates from October 1917. In the meantime, however, our aviation has made a significant step forward, especially in the fighting along the Western Front.

A small amount of rather fragmentary information has reached us. This consists of a few lines concerning tactics and procedures, but it is too imprecise for any conclusions to be drawn from it. There are also reports on new aircraft types.

Squadron activities, qualitative and quantitative conditions between the air forces of the individual states.

Our aviation industry is in no position to keep pace with that of the enemy. We are almost six months behind.

Now, in our state of isolation, this gap has increased to a year. We must be aware that we do not have any domestically-developed aircraft and that the types that we are flying are copies of English or French designs. Every possible effort must be made to communicate with the western aviation industry and achieve the production of new aircraft types.

This is the most urgent task facing our aviation industry.

Air Fleet Report No. 1/5 dated 1920

The Versailles Peace Treaty is the most devastating and unfair treaty ever forced upon a defeated nation. Germany, destroyed by war, was no more responsible for the outbreak of war than any of the other participating nations, however it is being completely plundered and exploited by this document.

It has lost tremendous military-technical potential and its fighting strength has been reduced to almost nothing.

Military aviation no longer exists and aviation must only serve cultural purposes.

All of Germany is subjected to surveillance from the air which covers almost every major city. Development of civilian aviation is under strict control.

Faced with constant fear of military aviation arising under a civilian cover, restrictions have been imposed which severely hamper the development and spread of civilian aviation.

Resolution by the Aviation Commissariat in the St. Petersburg District 17 September 1918

It is no secret that highly unreliable elements are commanders and pilots in the air fleet of our army of the workers and farmers class. The facts about the flights to the enemies of the working class carried out by Soviet pilots prove conclusively the existence of such elements within our comradely ranks. Even though a blind man can see that the Red Army is neither a band of robbers nor a small partisan unit, but the powerful armed force of an emerging nation, these people would rather serve the banditry of international capitalism.

It must be made clear to every pilot of the Red Army that flights to the criminals of the "White Garden", to the English or French of other elements, will have immediate consequences for friends and relations. These will also affect persons who have sponsored the pilots of such flights.

They should be aware that for each of them there are hostages, who will be called to account in keeping with the crimes. Every commander is required to read out this resolution and have his pilots signify its receipt with their signature. The signatures of absent or new pilots are to be submitted later. Lists of signatures are to be sent to the commissariat of the air fleet district.

Signed

Members of the council of Russian air fleets
Petr Zhuravsky
M. Savitzky

Albatros C I of a Russian aviation battalion.

Winter photograph of an LVG B I, also known as the "Flying Banana." The Russian insignia were applied to all wing undersides.

Pilots and mechanics pose in front of an Albatros C XII of a Soviet aviation battalion. Visible on the aircraft's rudder is the Red Star (with black outline). The aircraft's wheels have been replaced with skis for winter operations.

An Albatros C XII of a Red Army aviation battalion. The aircraft was painted pale grey overall, making the black outlined red stars stand out very clearly. Note that a red star has also been applied beneath the nose of the aircraft, which was non-standard. Further evidence of Soviet ability to improvise is the undercarriage, consisting of two conventional skis, a rather high-drag arrangement compared to the original streamlined undercarriage.

Standard Red Army markings consisted of national insignia on the upper and lower wing surfaces, as well as the fin and rudder, as seen here on a DFW C V. National insignia were not normally applied to the fuselage sides, however, there were exceptions to the rule.

LVG C V bombers in service with an aviation unit of the Red Army. These aircraft were supposedly purchased following the October Revolution, however, this cannot be confirmed. A number of these aircraft were stationed on the Turkestan Front in Central Asia, where this photo was probably taken, most likely in the 1920s.

At least one Friedrichshafen G IIIa fell into Russian hands and was later used as a personal transport by Lev Trotsky. The aircraft later made a crash-landing in Lithuania. This photo shows the aircraft undergoing repairs in a Lithuanian hangar. Following the completion of repairs, the aircraft continued to fly in Lithuania.

An LVG C VI after overturning on landing. The color scheme is typical of Soviet aircraft of the 1920s, with green upper surfaces, pale blue under surfaces, and a natural metal engine cowling. This aircraft may have been purchased with LVG C IIIs, IVs, Vs, and Vis, however, this cannot be confirmed.

An LVG C I still in the colors of the Russian air forces. The upper engine cowling and tires have been removed.

1922-1933

Following the German surrender at the end of the First World War and the revolutionary changes in Russia, the two states found themselves in a similar hopeless situation. The result was a gradual rapprochement for the purpose of assuring their respective interests.

The German-Russian Trade Treaty was signed on 16 May 1921. It was the start of a series of agreements and consultations which culminated in the Peace Treaty of Rapallo. The treaty was signed on 16 April 1922, and resulted in a resumption of diplomatic relations. It also settled the question of responsibility for the war and other controversies, smoothing the way for bilateral cooperation.

The start of cooperation in the field of aviation may be dated to 11 November 1921, the day the German-Soviet aviation company DEROLUFT was founded.

In the next three years the Soviets cultivated close contacts with Junkers, Dornier, and Heinkel. For the most part, the activities of the three companies had certain parallels with Russia. The greatest influence, however, was exerted by Junkers with its airline. Junkers aircraft were purchased in Germany and Sweden, and license production was begun in Fili near Moscow.

The aircraft were used to carry passengers, mail, and freight, and had a great influence on the secret German training school at Lipetsk, where they were used as test aircraft.

Junkers aircraft were the most common German types in the USSR in the 1920s. Heinkel aircraft did not appear until later, but saw wide service. They were only used in a military role, and several were used for training at Lipetsk. Heinkel also produced a catapult system that was adopted by the Russian navy.

Dornier's efforts were directed towards civil aviation, however, its Wal flying boats saw extensive use by the Russian military and in polar expeditions. Other German aircraft types were used by the Soviets in small numbers, however, they had little influence on the aviation industry.

One other aircraft company deserves mention, even though it was not German but was inseparably linked with the German air effort in the First World War. The company in question was Fokker.

Fokker aircraft appeared in Russia in large numbers, at the latest after the founding of DEROLUFT, and in the training role at Lipetsk.

Military Aviation

The first German aircraft reached the USSR in 1922 and were placed in military service. The Junkers F-13/Ju 13 was used as a communications, transport, and training aircraft, however, it was more widely used as a civilian aircraft than by the military.

Claims that the machines were used as heavy attack aircraft have no basis in fact. The type did fly several communications missions during the Moslem uprising in Central Asia.

Other types which saw military service were the Junkers Ju 20 (A-20), Ju 21 (T-21/H-21), and G-1 (K-30), Dornier Wal, and the Heinkel KR-1 (HD-55), I-7 (HD-37c), and He 5e. Only a few of these types were later used in civilian guise.

Approximately 40 Ju 20 reconnaissance aircraft were allocated to the Baltic and Black Sea Fleets. Ju 21 heavy fighters and reconnaissance aircraft also served in significant numbers until the late 1920s. Although the type also flew combat missions against the Basmachi in Central Asia, it does not appear to have achieved any historical significance.

The Junkers G-1 was the first Soviet heavy bomber, and approximately 20 machines were in service between 1926 and 1931. Several were later converted into passenger aircraft. Two Junkers K-47s were tested at the N II VVS test center in 1930. The aircraft had probably come from Lipetsk.

The Dornier Wal flying boat was purchased directly from the manufacturer and served as reconnaissance aircraft and bombers. Wal flying boats served in the USSR from 1926 until the late 1930s, and were also widely used in civilian guise.

Two Heinkel He 5e were procured in 1927. They were operated by the Yeisk Flying School.

To meet a requirement for shipboard aircraft, in 1930 the Soviets purchased 30 Heinkel He 55a without motors. They were later fitted with M-22 power plants. The type served as a shipboard aircraft until 1938.

In 1929 Heinkel sold two Type K-3 catapults to the Soviet Union. They were installed on the warships *Parijskaya* and *Krasny Kavkaz*. In 1930 a committee led by air force commander Alksnis, military engineers Kharlamov and Stoman, and test pilot Kozlov purchased two Heinkel HD-37c while in Germany. It was assumed that the German fighter would replace the Russian I-5 in frontline service. One of the aircraft crashed during spin trials at a Russian military airfield near Moscow. The pilot, V.O. Pisarenko, was able to parachute to safety.

The committee blamed Heinkel. As a result, Heinkel sent a company pilot to Russia, where he completed the spin trials.

It was discovered that the German operating instructions for the HD-37c contained an instruction which had not been included in the translation for the Russian handbook. Under the direction of N.N. Polikarpov the aircraft was modified, and the result was designated the I-7 (I = fighter).

As revealed by the Russian aviation historian V.B. Shavrov, the general configuration, dimensions, and armament of the I-7 were almost identical with the HD-37c. Nevertheless, the type cannot be considered a direct copy, but rather a design with a significant German influence.

The I-7 was built in quantity by the State Aircraft Construction Company (GAZ No. 1). The following is a list of yearly production figures for the I-7:

1931	2
3862	45
5793	18
7724	66

A total of 131 machines.

Although the aircraft remained in service for many years, it was not a milestone in Soviet aviation development.

The total number of German machines, or Soviet derivatives of German types (modified He 37c or Soviet-built Dornier Wal) that saw service between 1922 and 1933 was 360 to 390. A detailed list follows:

7764	Junkers Ju 20
7886	Junkers Ju 21
7909	Junkers JuG-1
ca. 80	Dornier Wal
7939	Heinkel KR 1
8006	Heinkel He 37/c/I-7
8008	Heinkel He 5e
20	Junkers Ju 13

Soviet statistics reveal that the Soviet aviation industry produced approximately 9,000 aircraft in the same period.

In 1925 German aircraft types made up 9% of the Soviet inventory (1,085 in total, including 78 Ju 21 and 17 Ju 20). By 1931 this figure had fallen to just 2% (67 of a total of 2,929 aircraft). On 1 January 1931 the following German types were in the Soviet inventory:

Junkers Ju 13	2 serviceable	1 unserviceable
Junkers Ju 20		5 unserviceable
Junkers JuG 1	2 serviceable	1 unserviceable
Junkers JuG 1 (seaplane)	8 serviceable	2 unserviceable
Dornier Wal	14 serviceable	6 unserviceable
Heinkel KR-1	19 serviceable	
Heinkel He 5e	1 serviceable	
Heinkel	2 serviceable	1 unserviceable
Albatros	2 serviceable	2 unserviceable

It is impossible to say to what degree these percentages were influenced by propaganda, however, the figures clearly reveal a steady reduction in foreign types as the Soviet aviation industry developed.

Civil Aviation

German aircraft were also widely used in civil aviation. They made possible the first scheduled air service over the expanses of the Soviet Union. In the early 1920s the air routes were served by airline companies. The four largest were DEROLUFT, JUNKERS LUFTVERKEHR, DOBROLET, and UKRVOZDUHPUT.

A German-Soviet airline was founded on 11 November 1921. A trade delegation from the RSFSR signed a covering agreement in Berlin. The governing body was Aero Union.

The German partners contributed a significant number of pilots and technicians. The Russians contributed infrastructure and leased aircraft. The business was run by two directors, one from each nation.

Flight operations began on 1 May 1922 on the 1,200-kilometer route between Königsberg and Moscow. By 1933 the number of routes had only been doubled. At that time the airline operated over the Berlin-Moscow and Berlin-Leningrad routes, a distance of 2,278 kilometers.

In the first six months of operation the airline completed 120 flights, carrying 290 passengers and covering 24,500 kilometers.

In 1933 the airline carried 7,425 passengers, 1,645 tons of freight, and 31.6 tons of mail while covering 1,183,000 kilometers.

DEROLUFT racked up similar numbers, although the figures vary depending on the source. This may also be due to the fact that DEROLUFT served the secret training base at Lipetsk. Training aircraft were also flown to Lipetsk under the DEROLUFT name.

In the beginning the Fokker F-III was flown on these routes, and later the Fokker F. V and Junkers F 13 (as well as several other types).

In spite of the extraordinary limitations it was forced to operate under, DEROLUFT's operations may be characterized as effective. The company had a firm place in the Russian airline system. DEROLUFT existed until 1937, and was supposed to have been reactivated following the friendship treaty signed in 1939.

Another independent company was JUNKERS LUFTVERKEHR, founded by Hugo Junkers. The company's first experimental flights were made on the occasion of the Nizhniy Novgorod exhibition in 1922, over the route from Moscow to Nizhniy Novgorod. At that time the airline was already operating in central and northern Europe.

In January 1923 the company reached an agreement with the government of the USSR for a service from Sweden to Iran, whose most substantial segment was Petrograd - Moscow - Kharkov - Rostov on Don - Novorossisk - Batumi - Tiflis - Baku. Other segments would be negotiated separately.

In 1923 the airline conducted flights from Moscow to Baku from 1 June to 1 October using eight Junkers F 13 aircraft. In that period they flew 141,000 kilometers, carrying a total of 1,231 passengers, 143 tons of freight, and 1,548 tons of mail.

The network of routes reached a length of 2,200 kilometers, however, it was modified after the first flights. After these changes the machines flew the route Rostov on Don - Mineralnye Vody, and on to Grozny and Baku, however, the main route remained Moscow - Kharkov - Rostov on Don.

Known Registration Numbers of DEROLUFT Aircraft

Fokker F III	RR1	rebuilt in 1925
	RR2	modified in 1925
	RR3	
	RR4	
	RR5	modified to Grulich VI/D.A.L. Fokker F III
	RR8	
	RR9	
	D-200	
	D-902	
Fokker F V	RR13	
Dornier Merkur	RR30	
	RR34	
	RR35	
	URSS 306	
	D-1076	
	D-1077	
	D-1079	
	D-1080	
	D-1081	

The airline extended itself further over Russia, the Ukraine, and the Caucasus. As planned, in 1924 the route was extended in both directions. In the north a link was established between Leningrad and Sweden, while in the south the segment Baku - Enseli - Tehran was initiated. In 1925 Junkers Luftverkehr sporadically flew the route Baku to Enseli (392 km).

On 1 April 1925 it was decided to merge Junkers Luftverkehr with the Deutsche Aerolloyd AG, resulting in a new airline, Deutsche Lufthansa.

Junkers used the F 13 exclusively in its operations in the USSR. The Junkers F 13 was used by other, smaller companies flying in the USSR. These included the Danziger Luftsport GmbH, whose machines were marked with two white crosses and the codes "Dz" or "D."

The F 13 was used by the Soviet companies Zakavia and Siblet. The latter remained in existence for just a brief time. In 1924 Zakavia served the route Batumi - Tiflis - Baku, while Siblet operated in Siberia.

The Ukrvozduhput company operated mainly Dornier aircraft. This initially insignificant airline began operations in 1923. By

1924 it was flying routes between Kharkov - Kiev, Kharkov - Rostov on Don, Kharkov - Odessa, and Kharkov - Moscow. The center point of the route system was Kharkov, then the capital of Soviet Ukraine.

The entire route system was 2,090 kilometers long in 1925. In 293 flights the company flew 160,079 kilometers and carried 1,003 passengers and 11,146 kg of freight (including 3,445 kg of mail). The types used were the Dornier Komet I, Komet II, and Komet III.

Soviet types also came into service, initiating a major conflict. New types were produced by the design team of K.A. Kalinin. At the same time Dornier offered its own types.

The opinions of the participating experts varied. Some advocated closing the Kalinin design bureau and purchasing Dornier aircraft, while others held the opposite view. In the end the Russian design team won out, and was ordered to complete its work. This incident took place in 1926.

Dornier offered the Dornier Merkur, a type already being flown by other companies, such as Deroluft and Dobrolet on the Moscow - Berlin route.

Dobrolet was formed on 17 March 1923, and an airline operating license was granted on 30 April. A number of publicity flights were carried out before regular operations were begun. Dobrolet initiated service on 15 July 1923 on the route Moscow - Ivanovo Voznesensk - Nizhniy Novgorod. The Moscow - Kazan and Tashkent - Alma Ata routes were added in 1924.

The aircraft covered 166,000 kilometers, transporting 620 passengers and approximately 11 tons of freight. In the same year Dobrolet explored new routes in Central Asia, and later in the Urals, Siberia, and the far north.

The route system grew rapidly. In just 8 months in 1928 the airline carried 10,100 passengers, 103 tons of freight, and 82.5 tons of mail while flying 2,500,000 kilometers. By 1923 Dobrolet was the largest Russian airline.

Aeroflot appeared on the scene in 1932 and absorbed all the national airline companies. It seems interesting today that a new airline (Ukrvozduhput) was formed in the Ukraine solely at the urging of Dobrolet.

The Dobrolet supervisory board became shareholders in the new company. Dobrolet used both Russian and German aircraft, with German types predominating in the early years. The following types were leased or purchased by the airline at various times: Junkers F 13/Ju 13; Junkers W 33/PS-4; Junkers G 24/K 30/JuG 1; and Dornier Merkur.

Records reveal that the percentage of non-Russian aircraft was 90% between 1924 and 1932. This represented 30% of the entire Russian inventory. Most were German transport aircraft, which were particularly well suited to the needs of the day.

The advent of the airlines brought with it a requirement for the creation of infrastructure, such as airfields and maintenance and training facilities. German specialists played a major role in this. Junkers contributed a large number of personnel to the effort. In 1922 approximately 75% of Deroluft's employees were German. By 1925 this figure had dropped to 50%. By 1926 only two German specialists remained, supervising twenty-five workers in the Kharkov repair facility.

In addition to carrying passengers, German aircraft were used for aerial photography, agricultural tasks, and training and propaganda flights. They also made an important contribution to opening the north.

O.A. Kalitzva flew a Junkers F 23 from the island of Wrangel. In 1925 Kalitzva and B.G. Chukhnovski flew a Junkers Ju 20 over the route Leningrad - Petrozavodsk - Arkhangelsk - Kolgnev - Matochkin Shav.

Junkers Ju 13 and JuG 1 aircraft took part in the search and rescue effort for the Nobile expedition. Two Junkers W 33/PS 4 aircraft participated in the rescue effort for the crew of the *Chelyuskin*.

The Dornier Wal served in the northern regions for a long time, where its excellent water characteristics and great endurance were particularly valuable.

Several German machines made noteworthy long distance flights. On 10 June 1925 a Junkers F 13 took off on a flight from Moscow to Peking.

In 1926 two Junkers G 24 aircraft overflew Russian territory en route from Berlin to Peking. The huge Junkers G 38 visited the Soviet Union on 22 September 1932 during its flight from Königsberg to Moscow.

The Junkers Branch Plant in Fili

In the face of economic problems, in the first half of the 1920s Soviet authorities withdrew somewhat from the militant communism of the civil war period. The new economic policy permitted small and medium private enterprise, including those by foreign investors.

In October 1919 a Junkers F 13 made a forced landing near Kovno in Lithuania. The pilot told the authorities that he was en route to Russia for preliminary negotiations for the sale of Junkers aircraft to Russia. On 12 December 1922 the People's Commissariat gave Junkers permission to establish facilities for the manufacture of aircraft and aero engines.

German authorities were also interested in production facilities for Duraluminum. The necessary documents were signed on 29 January 1923, and a supplementary agreement was signed in May 1924.

The establishment of the Junkers production facilities received a great deal of support from the *Reichswehr*. A monthly production rate of 300 aircraft was strived for, of which just 30% would remain in Russia. Production would be managed by German engineers and Russian specialists, who would receive exposure to all-metal construction for the first time.

Following the installation of all the necessary tools, production of BMW IIIa engines and Junkers Ju 20 and Ju 21 aircraft was begun. Production of the Junkers F 13/Ju 13 and JuG 1, which was also being built by the A.B. Flugindustri in Linham, began later. The number of employees stood at 1,350. Altogether, production totaled about 40 Ju 20, 122 Ju 21, 23 JuG 1, and several F 13/Ju 13.

If all the Junkers aircraft that were left in the USSR between 1923 and 1926 were in fact built at Fili, it would have had the following production rate:

1923	40 Ju 20, 40 Ju 21, 29 F 13	(109)
1924	53 Ju 21, 6 F 13	(59)
1925	26 Ju 21, 3 JuG 1, 6 F 13	(35)
1926	3 Ju 21, 12 JuG 1	(15)

In this case, production totaled 218 aircraft. Many aircraft entered service with the military and required a number of modifications.

In 1923 two Junkers F 13 were sold to Iran for reconnaissance and light bombing. They had cut-outs behind the cockpit for installation of machine-gun ring mounts. It may be assumed that the aircraft were diverted from Lipetsk and modified in Fili. The branch plant at Fili existed until March 1927, however, production had dropped off prior to this.

Junkers rejected a *Reichswehr* proposal to enter into cooperation with BMW for the license production of engines.

The *Reichswehr* ended its financial support of the Fili factory in 1925. Junkers ceased production of engines soon afterwards. With the end of support from the *Reichswehr*, the financial burden was assumed by the GUAP (Central Administration of the Aviation Industry). Sergei Gorbunov became the factory director.

In July 1926 a group of Russian technicians began work on the TB-1 heavy bomber. The aircraft was designed by A.N. Tupolev. Later Junkers and the TsAGI accused Tupolev of patent infringement in building the TB-1. The case went nowhere, however.

What was the reason for the rapid halt in license production? Cooperation between Junkers and the Russian authorities reached its apex between 1923 and 1924. There followed a steady decline until its ultimate cancellation in 1927. This applied similarly to Junkers aircraft and to the workshops in Fili, which in Junkers' view was the most important aspect.

The cancellation of the license agreement was followed by a steady decline, and business never again reached its former level, despite an attempt to revive it between 1928 and 1930.

The most likely reason was a turn toward the west, rather than a doubtful investment in an East European operation. For their part, the Soviets accused the Fili factory of having failed to live up to contractual obligations. There was even suspicion that a breaking of relations would be in the best interests of the Soviet Union.

A well-organized organization, highly-developed technology, and trained personnel remained in Fili, ready to begin production of Russian aircraft types.

Russian authorities discussed possible concessions relating to the use of private enterprise to build socialism. In the end the authorities made these concessions for two reasons: first, they urgently needed foreign capital to industrialize the nation; and second, they hoped to obtain the latest technology.

The School and Test Center at Lipetsk

The complete name of this installation was Scientific Research and Testing Establishment (Wivupal). The purpose of the institute was to circumvent the terms of the Versailles Treaty, which forbade military aviation in Germany.

Russian territory was closed to the victorious powers, and the vastness of Russia was an ideal place in which to conceal a secret installation. The interests of the Soviet Union matched those of Germany, which was interested in rebuilding its military power.

The first discussions took place in 1923 when *General* Haase met with a delegation from the USSR. *Sondergruppe Moskau* (Special Group Moscow), under the command of *Oberst* Lieth-Thomsen, was formed to continue the negotiations and maintain contact with the Soviet government.

In 1924 the first seven German officers were attached to Soviet air force units. The treaty which formed the legal basis of the agreement was signed in Moscow on 15 April 1925.

The treaty bore the signatures of the commander of the Red Fleet of the Worker and Farmer Classes (RKK-VF) P.I. Baranov and the director of Special Group Moscow, *Oberst* Lieth-Thomsen.

A Russian company, GEFU (Free Trade and Development Company), was formed to act as a cover for the development and manufacture of new aviation technology. The flying school was referred to in Soviet documents as the 4th Air Force Squadron RKKVF. All of these measures reflected the high degree of security attached to the program.

In spite of everything, however, neither party to the agreement was interested in a real exchange of information. Hundreds of NKVD agents were kept busy monitoring contacts between German and Soviet personnel. The result of this constant spying was that the only information available about the school took the form of legends, rumors, and rather doubtful speculation.

German personnel reached Lipetsk by sea or rail. All participants had false passports and names. Their names were also stricken from the *Reichswehr* personnel lists. Soviet uniforms were worn without rank badges. Weapons and equipment were transported to Leningrad in small ships.

Fifty Fokker D XIII formed the backbone of the training fleet. They were purchased from Fokker in the Netherlands. Later, aircraft were delivered by air with civil registrations under the Deroluft flag. From 1930 on several aircraft wore the codes of the Rechlin Test Center.

The test installation was commanded by *Major* Stahr. The first course for fighter pilots was held in 1925. From then until 1933 approximately 120 fighter pilots were trained at Lipetsk. Thirty of these were veterans of the First World War, while twenty were civilian pilots.

From 1928-1931 approximately 100 observers passed through the school. Four classes graduated per year, with each class consisting of six or seven pilots.

In summer the school's personnel complement climbed to approximately 200, while in winter it was reduced. 303 persons were reported in 1932, consisting of 43 German and 26 Soviet pilots, plus 234 ground personnel. In this way the personnel was mixed, and financing by the Soviet government was assured.

The exact number of Soviet specialists who passed through Lipetsk is not known, but by 1926 sixteen pilots and 45 mechanics had graduated for the Soviet air forces.

The relationship between the German and Soviet personnel can be characterized as friendly until the shutting down of the facility. The national anthems of both nations were played at all official functions.

Some of the graduates of Lipetsk rose to senior positions and returned to Russia after the outbreak of war:

Dessloch	*1. Flakkorps*, later commander of the *6.* and *4. Luftflotte*.
Fiebig	Richthofen's successor in the *8. Fliegerkorps*.
Pflugbeil	commander of the *IV. Fliegerkorps* and *Luftflotte 1*.
Plocher	Chief-of-Staff *V.Fliegerkorps*, later *Luftwaffenkommando Ost*.

A number of German personnel lost their lives in training accidents. The remains were placed in crates marked "machine parts" and transported to Germany. Customs personnel were alerted to prevent any embarrassing incidents at the border.

In June 1933 Jakov Berzin, head of the RKKA signals staff, reported to M.N. Tukhachevsky, Deputy Commissar for Military and Marine Affairs—who was also the overseer of German-Soviet cooperation in the military field—that two German Fokker F XIIIs had collided in midair during a training flight on 2 June. One pilot baled out at a height of 700 meters and survived. The second did not abandon his aircraft until a height of 50 meters and was killed. Both machines were destroyed.

Pilot Hans Karl von Treskov was killed in a crash on 9 September 1932. One year earlier pilot Emil Thuy was killed when the Albatros L 76 he was flying went down near Smolensk.

The school was visited by a number of high-ranking officers during its life:

Gen.Maj. von Blomberg,	Chief of the Army Department of the *Reichswehr*.
Gen.Maj. von Mittelberger,	Chief of the Organizational Department of the Air Force.
Major G. Felmi.	
Oberst Lieth-Thomsen,	Chief of the Special Group Moscow.

The school's structure was frequently modified to meet changing demands. The testing of various military aircraft began in 1928. The test department initially had between 50 and 100 personnel. Unlike the rest of the school, its main task was testing, not training. The unit had its own workshops, spare parts dump, ammunition stores, radio station, photo laboratory, and fuel dump.

Gunnery and bombing ranges were available near Voronezh, approximately 120 kilometers from Lipetsk.

In 1925 negotiations took place for the use of a naval air base near Odessa, however, these were broken off by the Germans.

As far as equipment goes, the trainer fleet remained relatively constant. The standard type was the Fokker F XIII. When the school closed in 1933 approximately thirty of these machines were handed over to the Soviet air force. Only one was flown to Germany. It bore the code D-2252.

Other types were used as advanced trainers and multi-purpose aircraft. These included the Fokker D VII, Junkers F 13 and A 20/35, Heinkel HD 17 and HD 21, and the Albatros L 76 and L 78.

The test unit flew a wide variety of aircraft, in most cases a single example of each type. Prototypes of fighter, bomber, reconnaissance, attack, and naval aircraft were intensively test flown.

As Lipetsk lacked a suitable body of water, marine aircraft could only be tested with a conventional undercarriage. Among the water-borne aircraft tested in this way were the He 59 and the Arado SSDI.

As sea trials were conducted in Germany, testing at Lipetsk was limited to weapons and tactics.

A complete list of the aircraft types flown at Lipetsk appears in the second volume in Appendix 5.

The Soviet reasons for opening the Lipetsk test center were revealed in a letter written by I. Unshilit, deputy head of the *Revvoensovet USSR*, in 1926:

1.) The school is creating an outstanding staff of specialists, technicians, and workers.
2.) It makes it possible to obtain the latest knowledge in various areas of aviation.
3.) Testing of weapons and equipment gives us insight into the latest technical innovations.
4.) The school provides an opportunity to train flight personnel and to steadily improve training.

The closing of the school in 1933 was predetermined by changes in the internal and foreign policies of the two partner states. Economic factors also played a role in the closure. Lipetsk was the most expensive German facility in the Soviet Union.

In addition to Lipetsk, Germany maintained a tank school in Kazan and a chemical warfare training school. There was therefore no reason to commit financial resources for other facilities. The Soviet Union also followed its own interests and acted accordingly.

Ja. Berzin, head of the Secret Service Department (RKKA), submitted a letter to K.E. Voroshilov, the People's Commissar for Defense, stating that the Lipetsk training center had not served the interests of the RKKA in the period until 1928.

This resulted in a project by the Central Committee (VKP (b)) concerning the relationship between the RKKA and the *Reichswehr*, with the objective of obtaining aircraft from Germany for training at Lipetsk and to conduct information gathering with the participation of Soviet personnel. In spite of everything, in the negotiations between Gen. Adams (head of the *Reichswehr*'s army group) and M.N. Tukhachevsky (head of the Aviation Department of the RKKA) (UVVS RKKA) in Moscow in 1931, the Germans avoided being drawn into a discussion about turning Lipetsk into a joint research and test facility.

From these discussions, the Soviet authorities came to the conclusion that the Germans were not interested in sharing the technical and tactical lessons being learned at Lipetsk.

The result was the gradual restriction and eventual closing of the German facilities by the Soviet authorities. A conference of the heads of the RKKA and the People's Commissariat (military and naval matters), chaired by Ja. Berzin, decided that:

1.) No further buildup of personnel at the German facility.
2.) Restriction of transfer of German specialists to territory of the USSR.
3.) No special tariff arrangements for the transport of German supply goods.
4.) No further use of the gunnery range for the German school.
5.) Reduction of Soviet personnel at the German school to a minimum.
6.) Formation of a liquidation committee.

As a result, the training center was closed in August-September 1933. On 31 August 1933 Berzin reported to Voroshilov that their "Friends" had abandoned the station between 20 and 30 September.

At that time the first three transports left the Soviet Union, and three aircraft belonging to the "Friends" departed for Germany on 29 August along the Deroluft air transport route. The transfer was completed without incident.

The estimated value of the materiel handed over to the Red Army was approximately 2.9 billion Reichsmark.

The end was unavoidable. The period of forced friendship was over. Later it would be characterized as the most fruitful period of cooperation between the two nations.

Appendix

Vestnik Vozdushnogo Flota
(Report by the Air Fleet No. 3/4 1920)

Negotiations with friendly states were held in Moscow with the objective of establishing a route network and issuing concessions for air transport companies. Soviet and foreign aircraft will take part in regular flights.

Summary of Dobrolet Publications 1923

In a ceremony on 15 July delivery was taken of the first aircraft purchased with Dobrolet start-up capital. The handover was made by representatives of the industry and consisted of acceptance and licensing flights. The names of the aircraft were *Presidium VSNKH*, *Chevonetz I*, and *Prombank*. In the coming days the *Mossovet II* would join its older brother flown in on 29 June.

Dobrolet purchased Junkers F 13 six-seat passenger aircraft in Germany. Seven aircraft were taken delivery of and placed in service. According to an agreement with Junkers, further machines were supposed to be delivered by 15 August at the latest and put into service for the summer season. Dobrolet was expecting to offer flights in Junkers aircraft to Vedenskoe, approximately 48 kilometers from Moscow. The service was intended to offer residents of the city the opportunity to get away to the forest near the river for rest and relaxation.

Dobrolet had established a flight school designed to meet the company's requirements. Training included aviation law, aerodynamics, systems technology, and so on. Research was conducted into aircraft and engine design and airline operations.

Publication of the Air Fleet No. 6/1923
Dobrolet at the 1st Agricultural Display of the States of the Soviet Union

On 5 August several pilots were assigned to search for suitable landing fields. Special attention was paid to the Moswa River, which was less than ideal for float aircraft.

In spite of everything, the basis for a water-based passenger service was established there. In just 20 days a seaplane base with associated buildings was set up. Land aircraft were equipped with floats (built and delivered by Junkers within 20 days).

By 25 August the aircraft *Prombank* was ready for service. With the director of Dobrolet on board, it took off on a twenty-minute flight which ended with a smooth landing at another site. In 54 days bad weather prevented flying on just 6 days.

The director of the floatplane base often received requests for flights exceeding the normal 15 minutes. Price was no object.

A total of 253 passenger flights were carried out with 778 passengers (20% of them foreigners). Total flying time was 68 hours, 18 minutes.

The Dobrolet board of directors had earlier received a visit from representatives of the Dornier Flugzeugwerke. The purpose of the visit was to complete a deal for the purchase of aircraft. Dornier was prepared to extend the necessary credit. The machines, with spare parts and replacement engines, were purchased for a long service life. At that time Dornier aircraft were being operated by Ukrainian companies.

On 15 November the Dobrolet machine Mosovet II took off from Nizhniy Novgorod for Kazan with an en route stop at Samara. The purpose of the flight was to help raise money for the air fleet. In spite of poor weather (rain and fog) the aircraft arrived at Samara on 15 November. On 18 November it flew on to Kazan. Total flying time was 9.5 hours.

Dobrolet received several proposals from German pilots for a combined air operation.

On 23 November three Junkers aircraft were delivered by rail. They are to begin service between Tashkent and Verny (Alma Ata). Service is expected to begin in January-February 1924.

On Sunday, 25 November the formal acceptance of new aircraft took place, attended by comrade Trotsky. Industry and office workers of the Worsted Trest factory ferried the aircraft *Krasny Kamvolschic* and *Nauka*. The latter machine was purchased with donations from various circles in the USSR. It is equipped with German radio equipment. The third new machine bears the name *Pravda*. All three aircraft are six-seat Junkers F 13.

With the coming of the first snows trials with skis were carried out.

Samiolot No. 1, 1926

At the end of June the aircraft *Vse y Aviahim* took off from Moscow to visit surrounding towns and cities. These included Nizhniy Novgorod, Cheboksary, Christopol, Sarapul, Usolie, Cherdyn, Kotlas, Arkhangelsk, Onega, Kargopol, Belozersk, Rybinsk, Kalyazin, and Tver.

The aircraft flew a total distance of 9,600 kilometers plus 8,400 kilometers in local flights, for a total distance of 18,000 kilometers.

The aircraft visited a total of 67 destinations and made 496 landings. 1,800 workers and farmers were taken aloft, and 1,920 kg of propaganda material were dropped. Total flying time was 176 hours.

The aircraft *Litzom K Derevne* visited Voronezh, Kalach, Stalingrad, Krasnoarmeisk, Enotievsk, Astrakhan, Guriev, Uralsk, Orenburg, Samara, Pokrovsk, and Lipetsk, flying a total of 157 hours. It covered 8,320 kilometers, plus another 7,750 kilometers in local flights (total of 16,070), visited 66 landing fields with 403 landings, and took 1,204 workers and farmers aloft. In addition, it dropped 1,600 kg of propaganda material.

The aircraft *Sibrevkom* arrived 40 minutes late at Semipalatinsk. As no one had ever seen an aircraft before, a crowd gathered at the landing field. The pilot was forced to attempt a risky maneuver, which resulted in a crash.

Samolet No. 2, 1926

The three Junkers aircraft *Litzom K. Derevne*, *Vsy y Aviyhim*, and *Sibrevkom*, flown by pilots Kopylor, Moiseer, and Jeske, performed extremely well. The aircraft flew 51,000 kilometers, visited 200 destinations, carried 4,340 passengers, and dropped 4,800 kg of propaganda material. Flown by pilots Kopylor and Moiseer, the aircraft *Litzom K. Derevne* and *Vsy y Aviyhim* flew the routes:

1.) Moscow - Tula - Oriol - Tambov - Penza - Murom - Vladimir - Moscow
2.) Moscow - Kaluga - Briansk - Tver - Moscow

Both routes were operated for months, and the service ended on 15 march after 4,000 kilometers had been flown. The same distance was flown on local flights.

Vestnik Vozdushnogo Flota No. 6, 1923
Deroluft expanded its activities in 1924. A new landing field is supposed to replace Kovno. Next year an all-weather service will be established on the Moscow - Königsberg route. One aircraft is to be fitted with radio equipment. As well, tests are to be made with new aircraft designs, such as an Albatros six-seater.

Vestnik Vozdushnogo Flota No. 6/7, 1924
The Moscow to Königsberg flights were resumed in May, with four flights per week at first—Tuesday, Wednesday, Thursday, and Saturday. Single passage costs 125 U.S. dollars. The price includes 5 kg of baggage. Each subsequent kilo costs 5 rubles.

Deroluft increased its frequency on the Moscow - Königsberg route beginning on 1 June. One return flight is made daily.

In an effort to increase passenger traffic, the price was reduced from 125 to 75 U.S. dollars.

Twenty percent of the proceeds were donated to the construction of the Lenin Mausoleum in memory of the immortal V.I. Lenin.

Samolet No. 2, 1926
The pilots' pay was no less than 174 rubles, and rose to 270 rubles for Dobrolet in Central Asia. On average 180 rubles in summer and 280 rubles in winter. The pilots also received flight pay, 2.5 to 6 kopeks per kilometer, flight engineers .75 to 3 kopeks per kilometer. The average for Dobrolet pilots is 500 to 600 rubles, and for Deroluft pilots 600 to 650 rubles.

Vestnik Vozdushnogo Flota No. 11, 1924
In memory of military pilot B.K. Velling.

On 18 November 1923 Red Air Force pilot Boris Konstantinovich Velling was killed in the crash of his Junkers aircraft. We will always remember his flights to Turkestan in the old LVG in 1917, in which he covered more than 2,500 kilometers.

His legendary flights in his Junkers from Moscow over the Caucasus Mountains at a height of 300 meters, over the Caspian Sea, on to Buchara, Khiva, the Aral Sea, over the coast to Kazalinsk, and on to Tashkent will never be forgotten.

During the return flight, "Boba" (Velling's nickname) flew from Orenburg to Moscow with just one refueling stop in Borisoglebsk.

Headquarters of the Air Fleet, Dessau, 1 December
We followed Velling's flights with great admiration. The news of his death has saddened us all.

We would like to express our deepest sympathy to the air fleet and to the family of the deceased.

Professor Junkers

Representatives of the Junkers company have just returned from Iran, where they concluded agreements for establishing a network of routes within Iran. The subject of the agreement was an initial route Baku - Enzeli - Tehran, with a later expansion to Bushir.

In this way a link has been established from Stockholm to Tehran, taking three days instead of the previous three weeks.

Halberstadt C V fighter aircraft. Twenty of these machines are believed to have been purchased in 1922. Note the original lozenge camouflage on the wing and tail surfaces.

Two Friedrichshafen G IIIa were used by Soviet aviation. One machine was flown to Russia by German pilots with medicines, while the other was purchased in 1922.

LVG at Petrograd airfield in 1922. The aircraft bears no markings and still has the factory-applied lozenge finish.

Pilot Blagodelsky did a good job of disassembling this LVG C VI in Smolensk (1923). Note the fabric strips on the wings, covering the seams where the lozenge fabric was attached to the ribs. An idyllic scene in a Russian winter.

This LVG C V overturned after a forced landing.

Crashed LVG C V. The red star is visible on the fuselage side. In some cases wooden wheels replaced the original rubber tires.

Pilots and mechanics of the 20th Aviation Battalion. The photo was taken on 30 August 1922.

LVG C V of the 14th Aviation Battalion with pilots and mechanics. The aircraft was dark green with red stars on the wings and fin.

Instructor E.F. Burche and student pilot M.D. Ermolaev in the cockpit of an LVG C V.

Group photo in front of a Rumpler C IV in Petrograd in 1922. The observer holds the camera in a heroic pose. In the background is a Fokker D VII.

Pilot and observer in front of a Rumpler C IV, Petrograd 1922. Note the excellent condition of the machine and the modified windscreen for the observer.

A Rumpler C IV taxis at Petrograd, 1922.

Crashed Rumpler C IV at Komendantsky airfield.

Another wrecked Rumpler C IV. The crew (pilot Kuleshov) survived the accident. A machine-gun was installed in the observer's position. The aircraft still wears its original lozenge finish, and the German markings were simply overpainted (probably in red). These overpainted markings were seen on other aircraft.

A guard watches over an LVG V VI with unusual markings, probably a red cross on a white field. This aircraft may have been used to deliver medicines to Russia in 1920.

The famous pilot Velling (left) in front of his LVG C V in Turkestan. Following the collapse of the Central Asian front several aircraft were used to maintain an air link between Tashkent and Verny (Alma Ata).

Halberstadt C V flown by L. Popov after a crash in May 1924.

Crash landing by pilot Medvedev at Komendantsky airfield, Petrograd. The landing was so heavy that the port undercarriage was driven through the wing.

German aircraft damaged during training flights by the 1st Aviation Battalion. The photo was taken in Petrograd in 1922.

Российское Общество Добровольного Воздушного Флота

„ДОБРОЛЕТ"

Устав утвержден Совнаркомом 30 Апреля 1923 г.

Основной капитал 2.000.000 руб. золотом.

Цена акции 1 руб. 05 коп. в 52 руб. 50 коп. золотом по курсу Котировальной Комиссии в день взноса. Подписки на акции продолжается.

ВОЗДУШНОЕ СООБЩЕНИЕ по ЛИНИЯМ: МОСКВА ИВАНОВО-ВОЗНЕСЕНСК НИЖНИЙ НОВГОРОД.

Вместо 14 часов в душном вагоне—3 часа в уютном „Юнкерсе".

Принимается перевозка почты, посылок и проч. грузов.

Отправление регулярно из Москвы в 8 ч. ут., из Нижн.-Новгорода в 6 ч. веч.

Правление Об-ва: МОСКВА, Биржевая пл. д. 2-7. Тел. 216-72 и 216-78.

Московская Авио-станция — Ходынка, против Петровского Дворца.
Телефон 249-50.

Advertisement by the Russian airline Dobrolet. The flyer offers service from Moscow to Ivanovo and Voznesensk to Nizhniy Novgorod, promising three hours in a comfortable Junkers instead of fourteen hours in a dusty wagon. The aircraft were scheduled to depart Moscow at 8 PM and Nizhniy Novgorod at 6 PM, and mail, packages, and other freight could also be carried.

ЦЕЛЬНО-МЕТАЛЛИЧЕСКИЕ ПАССАЖИРСКИЕ АЭРОПЛАНЫ

ЮНКЕРС

заводов Юнкерс в Дессау (Германия).

Представительство в России: Москва, Петроградское шоссе, 32, тел. 10-77.

С 1 июня этого года О-вом ЮНКЕРС открывается воздушная линия:
Москва—Харьков—Ростов—н Д.—Новороссийск—Батум—Тифлис
Баку—Тегеран.

Advertisement by Junkers Luftverkehr for the opening of the air route Moscow - Kharkov - Rostov on Don - Novorossisk - Batum - Tiflis - Baku - Tehran.

Dornier Komet bearing the name Krasny Khimik (Red Chemists), registration R-RUAD operated by Ukrvozduhput. Komet I and II aircraft were flown by the Ukrainian airline. The two versions differed in the type of engine installed, either a BMW IIIa or Rolls-Royce.

Brand new Komet II with Rolls-Royce engine.

Another Dornier Komet operated by Deroluft with the registration RR 16. Note the legend "Moscow" on the ladder next to the aircraft.

Fokker F III operated by Deroluft with the registration RR 1.

This Fokker F III with the registration RR 4 was also operated by Deroluft.

Rare photo of a Deroluft Fokker F III during takeoff.

The Komet III's successor in service with Ukrvozduhput was the Dornier Merkur. Illustrated here is a Deroluft machine with the registration D-1081.

Dornier Komet with the registration CCCP-11. The aircraft is equipped with skis.

Dornier Merkur operated by Dobrolet. The legend Tz.O.K.P. Pravda means: Central Organ of the Communist Party "Pravda."

Loading mail sacks into Dornier Merkur CCCP-L74. The cockpit is glazed, and the exhaust has been modified. Curiously, the aircraft has no markings on the wing upper surface. The marking on the GAZ-AA truck is *Pochta* (mail).

Postcard put out by the airline Deroluft depicting a Dornier Merkur. Note the absence of registration.

Dornier Merkur operated by Deroluft. The fourth person from the right is the famous Russian writer Maxim Gorky.

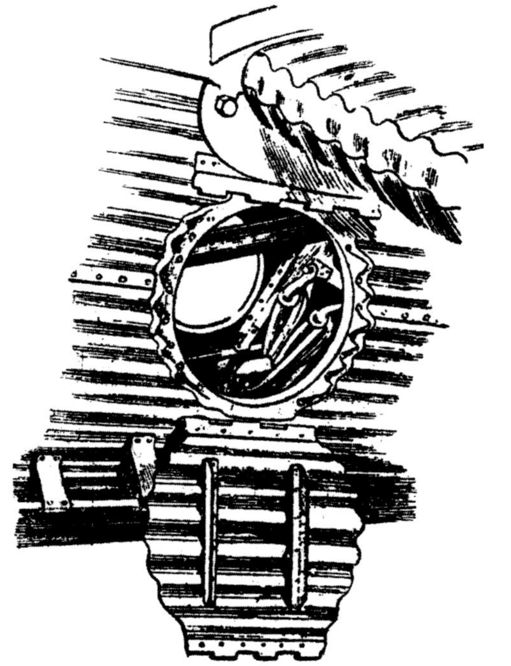

Рис. 4. Открывающаяся в хвосте фюзеляжа дверца, позволяющая видеть амортизатор костыля.

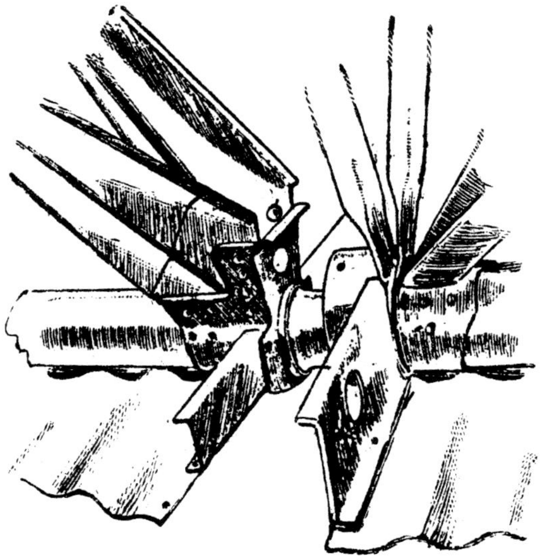

Рис. 2. Лонжероны внешних частей крыльев присоединяются к лонжеронам средней части крыла с помощью стальных гаек.

Рис. 3. Заключенное в крыле коромысло, передающее движение от тяги, управляемой пилотом, к кронштейну элерона.

Pages from a Russian maintenance manual for the Junkers F 13.

Junkers F 13s of Junkers Luftverkehr at Khodynskoe airfield, Moscow, in 1923. These aircraft flew the Moscow to Tiflis route.

An unidentified Junkers F 13 of Junkers Luftverkehr during operations in 1923.

A Junkers F 13 on approach to land at dusk, somewhere in Russia.

Junkers F 13 with the registration CCCP L-24 following a crash-landing. Note the long exhaust collector and the wooden propeller. One can only speculate as to the purpose of the wooden slats on the face of the radiator. In all likelihood the radiator proved too large for Russian temperatures. The slats helped reduce frontal area, helping the engine to reach optimal operating temperature.

The Junkers F 13 Pravda following a crash.

The BMW engine of the Junkers F 13 *Krasny Artelschik* following a crash-landing. Note the bent engine mounts and crushed radiator.

Junkers F 13 with the registration D 202 in front of a typical Russian wooden hangar. This aircraft may have been operated by Junkers Luftverkehr.

Junkers F 13 with the registration D 205 in flight.

Junkers F 13/Ju 13 wearing the two white crosses of the Free City of Danzig. This suggests that the aircraft belonged to Danziger Luftpost. According to the Swedish aviation historian Lennart Anderson, the aircraft belonged to Junkers and the Danzig markings were applied to prevent its possible confiscation by the Allied Control Committee.

This crash-landed F 13 also wears the Danzig markings.

Above: Junkers F 13 Prombank operated by Dobrolet. From August to September 1923 the aircraft made flights for the agricultural exhibition. The aircraft was probably flown by pilot Kiessner. Dobrolet took delivery of the machine on 15 July 1923, with registration RR-DAE. Note the R repeated on the fin.

Right: Junkers Ju 13 of Dobrolet with the registration RR-DAT. The aircraft's name cannot be identified.

Crash-landing by Junkers Ju 13 RR-DAA.

Junkers Ju 13 Krasny Kamvolschik, registration RR-DAO. In the background is the Ju 13 Pravda.

This Junkers F 13 made a forced landing after suffering engine failure, resulting in a collapsed undercarriage.

A Junkers Ju 13 in service as a propaganda aircraft. The aircraft's registration is not known. This is probably a posed photograph, supposedly depicting members of a collective farm presenting gifts to the crew.

Junkers Ju 13 R-RECF during an en route stop. This machine was formerly registered D-214 (serial number 630) Dompfaff.

Mossovet, a Junkers operated by Dobrolet, with the registration URSS-145. This photo was probably taken in Buryat (Mongolia) during operations as an agricultural spray plane. Note the spray equipment beneath the fuselage.

Crew and ground personnel pose for a souvenir photo in front of a nameless Junkers Ju 13 operated by Dobrolet. The aircraft, registration URSS 144, has been tied down to prevent storm damage.

Above: This crashed Junkers Ju 13 (RR-?DB) bears several interesting inscriptions: Agitsamoliot DVF (propaganda aircraft of the DVF) and Vse v O.D.V.F. The aircraft's name is Krasny Artelschik.

Right: Photograph of the same aircraft from another angle reveals the extent of the damage. The machine may have been a write-off.

Junkers Ju 13 with the legend Vse v Aviakhim - Samolet Aviakhim RSFSR. The aircraft was used for propaganda flights. Note the design of the skis with auxiliary fins.

Junkers Ju 13 *Krasny Komvolschik* operated by Dobrolet. The inscription on the photo reads: "First mail flight from Kazan to Moscow, 5 July 1924."

Bukharski Uli, a Dobrolet Ju 13 operated in Central Asia. The meaning of the legend in Arabic is not known.

Float-equipped Junkers Ju 13 with the registration RR-DAN and the name TzeKuBu.

Right: In 1925 pilots A.I. Babushkin and M.S. Babushkin flew Junkers Ju 13 *Prombank* to the North Pole. The aircraft was equipped with skis. Beneath the cockpit is the emblem of the Soviet Union.

Junkers Ju 13 *Pravda* after a crash-landing.

Above: Junkers Ju 13 Krasny Kamvolschik (RR-DAO) photographed during its record-setting flight from Moscow to Peking on 10-17 July 1925.

Right: This photo proves that there was a second Junkers Ju 13 with the name *Mossovet*. The differences between the two are not known.

Below: It is interesting that there was a second machine that carried the emblem of the Prombank (RR-DAE), this time named *Latyshsky Strelok*.

Above: In 1926 pilots V.L. Galyshev and F.I. Groshev flew the Ju 13 *Mossovet* along the Enisey River from Krasnoyarsk to Turukhansk and back.

Right: Junkers Ju 13 *Mossovet* (RR-DAA) with engine running. In 1927 the machine was used on the Buryat (Mongolia) route, along with the aircraft *Mostorg*, *Pravda*, and *Gosplan*.

Junkers Ju 13 marked with the number "1" of a Soviet aviation unit in Central Asia.

Above: In 1925 pilot Zakharov crash-landed this Junkers Ju 13 somewhere in Central Asia. By this time the red star had been adopted as a military marking.

Right and below: These two photos depict a Junkers Ju 13 with the unusual registration D 257. Although the marking appears to be civilian, the red star on the rudder suggests that it was operated by the military.

These three photographs depict another Junkers Ju 13 in service with the Soviet military. In the top photo one can see the steps on the port wing root, as well as handgrips and an inspection hatch on the aft fuselage.

Junkers Ju 13 Pravda in service as a passenger aircraft in Buryat, Mongolia, in 1927. The interesting collection of people makes the aircraft appear unusually large.

Junkers Ju 13 Sibrevkom with the registration RR-DAM (serial number 590) in Altai, probably in 1924. Note the unpainted wooden propeller.

Junkers Ju 20 seen being hoisted aboard the cruiser *Profintern*. The military code "2" and the small banner on the fuselage identify the aircraft as belonging to the Baltic Fleet.

Another photo depicts the Ju 20 after landing while approaching the cruiser *Profintern*. The observer stands ready to catch the crane hook while boats stand ready to assist.

Rare in-flight photo of a Junkers Ju 20, the same aircraft as in the previous photographs. The aircraft undersides were pale blue, whereas the floats were painted green overall. The design combined a wing with straight leading and trailing edges with typical convex Junkers ailerons.

This souvenir photograph depicts a group of Finnish and Swedish pilots who had emigrated to the Soviet Union. The Ju 31 on which the men are sitting belonged to the 31st Air Reconnaissance Battalion under the command of Chukhonovsky. The photograph was taken at Oranienbaum, near Leningrad, in 1925. Among the pilots seen here were Walter Bergstrem, Otto Kalvitza, Lathimiak, Karel Keronnen, Valtonen, and Renkas.

Aerial photo of the Gora Valdai seaplane base in the mid-1920s. Visible in the photograph are aircraft "3," "4," "6," and "8."

Above: Junkers Ju 20 during the period of the Arctic flights in 1924-25.

Right: Junkers Ju 20 photographed in the Far North. B.G. Chukhnovsky and O.A. Kalvitza (one of the Finnish pilots) flew this aircraft in 1924-25. Note that the observer's machine-gun has been removed.

Below: Junkers Ju 20 flown by pilot Kalvitza, seen here on the island of Gutuevski, Leningrad, in 1925.

Approaching the ship's crane. The observer of this Ju 20 is already standing on the wing in preparation for hoisting the aircraft aboard the ship.

Right: Junkers Ju 20 of an Arctic expedition after returning from a research flight. The aircraft receives an enthusiastic welcome.

Below: The well-known Soviet pilot O.A. Kalvitza in the cockpit of his Junkers Ju 20. A souvenir photograph with ground personnel.

A souvenir photograph on a Junkers Ju 20. The identities of the persons on the aircraft are not known.

Servicing a Junkers Ju 20 somewhere in the far north. Note the machine-gun mount in the aft cockpit.

Above: Another widely-used aircraft type was the Junkers PS-4, seen here during flight trials at the NII GVF test center.

Center: Junkers PS-4 at the NII GVF test center in 1934. Note the unusual wheel spats and the fully enclosed cockpit.

Right: Junkers PS-4 bearing the legend Aeroflot.

PS-4 in service in Siberia (registration USSR L-735).

PS-4 in service in Siberia. Here an engine change in bitter cold.

One of the two PS-4s that took part in the effort to rescue the crew of the *Cheljuskin*.

Changing the engine of a Junkers PS-4.

This Junkers PS-4 was also part of the effort to rescue the crew of the Cheljuskin. The radiator was covered because of the cold.

Junkers PS-4 after a landing accident. Unlike other aircraft of this type, this machine has a metal propeller.

Above: Two Junkers PS-4s in service in the Polar region. The registration of the machine in the background is SSSR-N5.

Right: Engine changes appear to have been the order of the day. Here the Junkers L-5 engine of a float-equipped PS-4 is being replaced.

Below: Float-equipped version of the PS-4 with the registration SSSR-175. Note the Latin letter "R" on the aircraft's rudder.

Passengers board a Junkers PS-4. Note the Junkers emblem to the right of the door.

Float-equipped Junkers PS-4 with the registration SSSR-L-735. Engine maintenance in the field.

Above: Junkers PS-4 registration SSSR-L-1415 at the Irkutsk seaplane base.

Right: SSSR-L-1414, a Junkers PS-4, taking off from a lake in the Siberian taiga.

Below: An interesting job for the Irkutsk seaplane base was repairing PS-4 SSSR-L-735, which sustained heavy damage in a landing accident.

Above: Junkers G 24 powered by two wing-mounted Junkers L-5 engines and one nose-mounted BMW VI engine.

Right: Arrival of the Junkers G 24, registration D 543 on 9 April 1925. The aircraft went on to make record flights with the registration RRECL.

Below: This bomber version of the Junkers JuG 1 was crash-landed at the Lukashino rail station by pilots Fiodorov and Potapov on 31 December 1930.

Two civilian Junkers JuG 1s with the registrations L-82 and L-83. Note that L-83 has had its fin and rudder removed.

Junkers JuG 1 in civilian use (registration SSSR-L-54). The machine had previously served with the military, as the machine-gun position reveals.

Junkers JuG 1 with the registration SSSR-L-82. Note the small landing flaps in the extended position.

Assembling the Junkers JuG 1 "Red Bear," Beverly Sound, 7 July 1928.

Pilot B.G. Chukhnovsky in front of a Junkers JuG 1 after a flight in the polar region. The photo was taken in the early 1930s.

A float-equipped Junkers JuG 1 sits on a calm lake waiting for its next flight.

Nice detail shot of a float-equipped Junkers JuG 1. Note the design of the landing flaps and the foot rests for the pilot, a typical Junkers feature.

Junkers JuG 1 with the registration SSSR-N-4. The armed and manned machine-gun position suggests that this was probably a military aircraft. Note the arrangement of the float struts, imparting an impression of sturdiness.

The aft section of the JuG 1 illustrated above. A large number of people was required to hold this large aircraft in position against the waves.

Above: This photo captures the atmosphere of water-borne operations in the pre-war period.

Below: Two more photographs of the JuG 1 illustrated on the previous page (SSSR-N-4).

The following series of outstanding photographs depict the Junkers JuG 1 *Red Bear* flown by the research pilot Chukhnovsky on board the icebreaker *Krasin*. The caption on the photograph reads "Norwegian fiord, 26 June 1928."

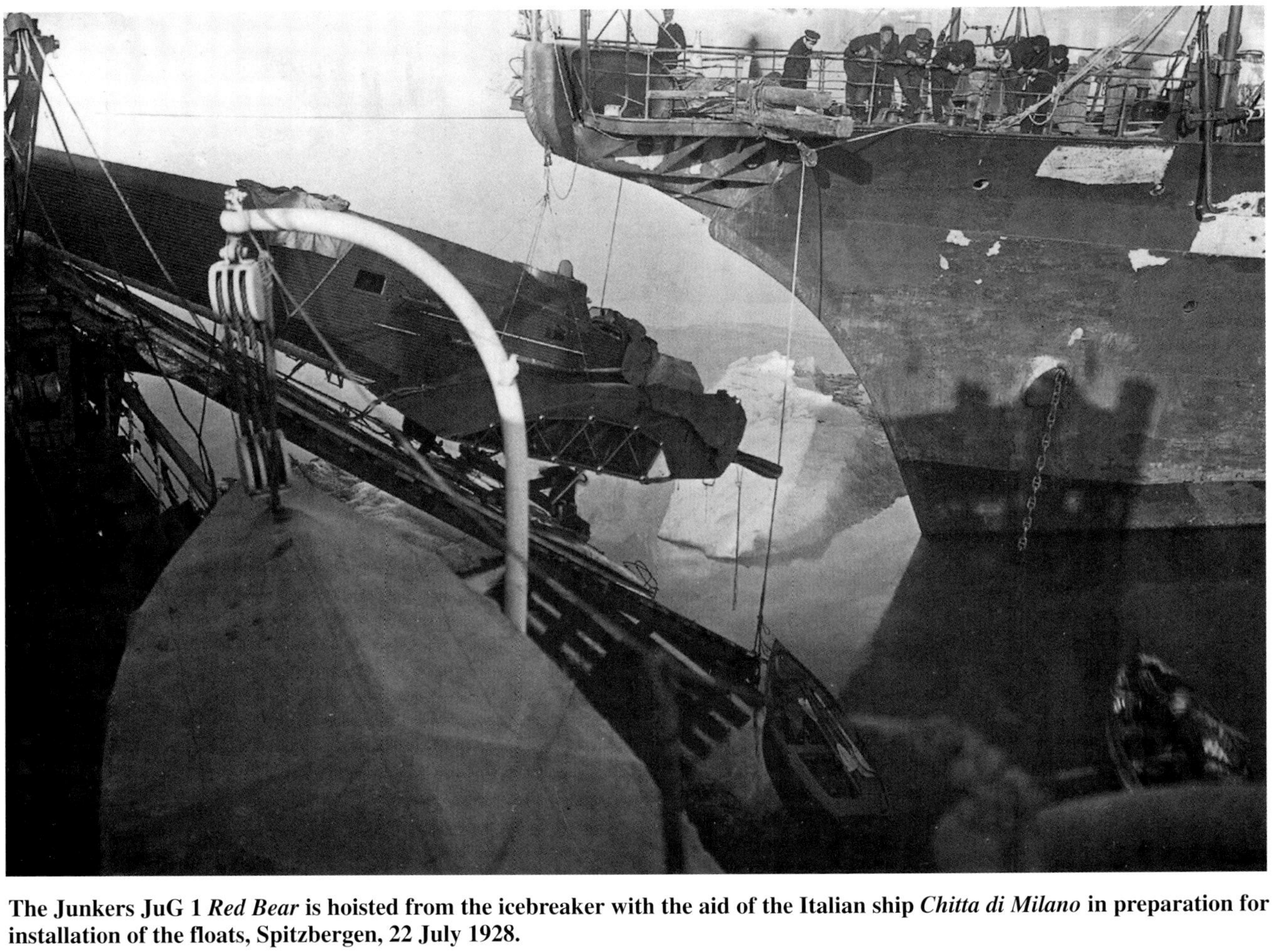

The Junkers JuG 1 *Red Bear* is hoisted from the icebreaker with the aid of the Italian ship *Chitta di Milano* in preparation for installation of the floats, Spitzbergen, 22 July 1928.

The machine suspended from the bow of the Italian vessel. The large floats have been moored to the anchor chain. This was a very time-consuming operation requiring a great deal of improvisational skill.

B.G. Chukhnovsky in the cockpit of his Junkers JuG 1 *Red Bear* with matching flag. The aircraft retained its military finish, dark green upper sides and pale blue under sides (see color plate).

The end of the research flights. The Junkers JuG 1 *Red Bear* is taken on board on 15 September 1928. The aircraft's wings have already been removed. This time the machine was taken aboard with its floats still in place.

In preparation for hauling the machine aboard, it has been positioned in front of the ramp tail-first with ropes attached to prevent drift.

The aircraft at the top of the ramp in the final phase of loading aboard the icebreaker *Krasin*.

Above: Soviet aircrew pose for a group photo in front of a Junkers JuG-1. Unlike the G 24, the JuG 1 was powered by three Junkers L-5 engines.

Center: Junkers JuG 1 about to touch down during a military exercise by the Leningrad Military District.

Below: High-ranking Soviet officers photographed with a JuG 1. In the center, wearing a grey military coat, is Peoples Commissar for Defense K.E. Voroshilov. Far right is the head of the test center P.I. Baranov wearing a light summer blouse.

Above: Archive photograph of a Junkers Ju 21 with the legend *Tiumensky Krest'yanin*. The photo was taken in Central Asia in the mid-1920s.

Center: The Junkers Ju 21 aircraft of the 2nd Aviation Battalion on parade. The top panels of the engine cowlings and machine-guns have been removed on account of the high temperatures. These aircraft were used mainly for reconnaissance.

Below: Group photograph in front of a Junkers Ju 21. Note the machine-gun on the ring mount in the observer's cockpit.

This souvenir photo of an AV pilot reveals a number of details of the Junkers Ju 21. Note one of the two machine-guns above the engine. The weapon bears a certain similarity to the German MG 08/15.

Camera-equipped version of the Junkers Ju 21 after a survey flight. Note the damage to the fin and rudder.

Crash-landed Junkers Ju 21 at Karshi, Central Asia, 1925-26. The aircraft was piloted by Frantzev.

This Junkers Ju 21 made a crash-landing near the Samsonovo rail station in 1924. Note the jettisonable fuel tank, which sustained minor damage in the crash.

Another view of Frantzev's Ju 21. An armed guard watches over the aircraft.

This photograph might be titled "Nature and Technology." The Central Asian steppe provides an eerie background for technical inadequacy. This is the same Ju 21 illustrated above and on the previous page.

Another German aircraft that saw many years of service in the USSR was the Dornier Wal. This photograph depicts a Wal of the Black Sea Fleet being prepared for a routine flight. Note the dolly wheels floating on the beach.

Takeoff from Sevastopol. Armed with bombs, a pair of Dornier Wal seaplanes takes off on a patrol.

The Dornier Wal *Sovetsky Sever* was the aircraft of pilot Volynsky. Here it is seen taking off from Petropavlovsk harbor in July 1928. The aircraft bears no markings.

Dornier Wal with the registration SSSR-N-1.

Above: The Dornier Wal flown by pilot Molokov. Note the DF loop on the fuselage nose. The aircraft's registration is SSSR-N-2.

Center: A pair of Dornier Wal flying boats in flight over the Black Sea.

Below: Dornier Wal No. 1 Severput on an improvised dry-dock.

Above: Dornier Wal SSSR-N-2 in a very "low-tech" hangar. The rugged conditions do give some indication of the design's robustness and reliability, however.

Center: A crew of men restrains pilot Chuknovsky's Dornier Wal as it is rolled toward the water.

Below: Dornier Wal SSSR-N-2 undergoing repairs.

Above: Molokov's Dornier Wal was modified to meet his own requirements.

Center: Another photograph of Dornier Wal SSSR-N-1 during flight operations.

Below: Dornier Wal SSSR-N-4 during takeoff.

The crew of Dornier Wal *Severput No. 1* pose for a photograph.

Group photograph on a Wal.

The propeller had to be turned by hand several times prior to engine start. This lubricated the pistons and prevented the engine from turning over dry while starting.

Dornier Wal test commission in Sevastopol in the late 1920s. Note the bulky nose turret.

A small boat tows a Dornier Wal to shore while the crew stands on the sponson.

Dornier Wal on an internal Soviet waterway. A crowd of interested onlookers has gathered to watch the aircraft.

The two photos above depict the Dornier Wal of the well-known pilot Alexeev.

Forward view of the Wal engine with propeller removed. Note the Bollard thermometer on one of the engine struts and the covered pitot tube.

Rear view of a Wal engine. Note the design of the propeller attachment plate.

Soviet Dornier Wal with the registration SSSR-N-1 is put into the water. This aircraft was stationed in the Arctic. Note the simplicity of the seaplane base, which in that remote region surely did not offer a very high standard of living.

Dornier Wal with the registration SSSR-N2 takes off from an interior waterway. The well-known pilot V.S. Molokov flew this aircraft on the Krasnoyarsk to Moscow route from 22 July to 19 September 1936.

Molokov's aircraft during preparations for takeoff. The aft engine has already been started.

The same machine at its moorings. The significance of the funeral flowers is not known.

Three photographs of Dornier Wal SSSR-N8, flown by S.A. Levanevsky on the Sevastopol - Khaborovsk route.

Dornier Wal SSSR-N10 at a seaplane base in the Arctic.

The same machine is placed in the water with engines running.

Dornier Wal SSSR-N8, the aircraft of Levanevsky, moored at the mouth of a stream.

This Dornier Wal bore the unusual registration SSSR-N237 at the beginning of the 1940s.

A Dornier Wal at an Arctic station in the mid-1940s. By this time the Wal had been replaced in service by more modern aircraft, such as those visible in the background.

The same Dornier Wal. The aircraft is apparently being disassembled, with the forward engine already removed.

A Dornier Wal flying boat of the Black Sea Fleet, stationed in Sevastopol. In some respects the aircraft's equipment is unusual. Note the two wind deflectors in front of the rear gun position and the bombs hung on the side of the fuselage. The flight engineer is performing final engine checks before takeoff.

Two photos which capture the atmosphere of flying boat operations in Sevastopol harbor.

Installing wheels on the sponsons of the Dornier Wal was a laborious process.

The end of a Wal. The stripped-down remains of the Wal bearing the name *Sovetsky Sever* were hauled ashore on the north coast of Kluchinskaya Guba Bay to await scrapping.

1934-1939

The development of Soviet-German relations in the 1930s were characterized by the growth of two major powers that exclusively pursued national interests. Thus, by 1934 all that was left of the once close cooperation in the field of aviation was passenger flights by civilian aircraft.

In spite of this, in the mid-1930s there was a deepening of the business relationship with the Heinkel company. The negotiations concerned the procurement of shipboard catapults for the new KDR-1 shipboard observation aircraft, which was still in development.

Heinkel required precise technical specifications for the aircraft in order to develop a suitable catapult. The Soviet authorities were hesitant because of security, and because not all the data was available at that time.

A year of fruitless correspondence finally resulted in the ordering of K-12 catapults. In May 1939 one of these, a K-12B, was installed on the cruiser *Voroshilov*. The second catapult, a K-12A, was installed on the cruiser *Kirov* in August of the same year.

In June 1939 Heinkel submitted an offer to the USSR to sell the plans for the K-12 catapult for 300,000 Reichsmark, provided at least three catapults were purchased. This deal fell through for various reasons.

After 1933 the Soviets monitored German aviation developments from secret service sources, open investigation, and other sources. The Spanish Civil War changed this situation abruptly. Suddenly, German and Soviet aircraft were facing each other in the air. It soon became obvious that the German machines possessed superior performance to their Soviet counterparts. There were areas, however, where they were inferior. The Soviets made a determined effort to acquire examples of German warplanes. The war provided the necessary opportunities, and the Soviets acquired examples of at least three different machines for inspection: the He 51 A, Messerschmitt Bf 109 B, and Heinkel He 111 B.

Two He 51 A fighters turned up in Moscow. How they got there is not known for certain, however, they attracted a great deal of interest. The type provided no surprises, and the Soviets reached the conclusion that the type was obsolete.

The Bf 109 was a different story. It was a new generation fighter, and its way to the Soviet flight test center is an interesting story.

On 4 December 1937 a Bf 109 B (6-15) flown by Fw. Polenz ran out of fuel and made a forced landing on the road between Azaila and Escatron. At about the same time a Heinkel He 111 B (52-32) fell into Republican hands. These two machines served as trump cards in negotiations with the French, who were interested in exchanging military supplies for captured German aircraft.

On 31 January 1938 a secret French delegation visited Barcelona and examined the Bf 109. The machine was subsequently shipped to Odessa, and then taken by train to Moscow. When it arrived at the test center (N II VVS) the aircraft bore no markings.

The Soviets initially carried out ground tests, as revealed by the following extract from a report dated 14 April 1938:

...initial results of ground trials with the Bf 109 B—Jumo 210 power plant (engine number 156)—on 14 April 1938 reveal a high degree of design quality....

The report subsequently dealt with technical details and materials, which were undoubtedly of great interest to Soviet industry and the military.

The report lauded the type's ease of handling, the well thought out construction, the weapons installation, general equipment, and ease of servicing under field conditions.

The equipment industry was urged to closely examine the machine's general equipment and to incorporate items of interest in Soviet production. The following items were of particular interest:

Oxygen system and tank
Oxygen system fittings
Oxygen mask of frost-proof synthetic material
Various electrical switching elements
Undercarriage and tailwheel design
Hydraulic systems

The He 111 B also visited the USSR, however, it was not tested extensively, as the authorities satisfied themselves with the Russian translation of the French test report. The general tenor of the report was not as favorable as the Soviet assessment of the Messerschmitt:

Good basic aerodynamic design
Sturdy design, somewhat obsolescent and too heavy
General technology too complicated and outdated
Design of the outer wings outdated and skinning too thin
Basic design of relatively simple nature, however not absolutely simple in detail, rather too complicated
Only the equipment and armament can be seen as modern.

The report had the following to say about the type's military usefulness:

Internal equipment very well laid out and good comfort for the crew
Some elements of the design are excellent
The crew arrangement requires good intercom coordination
In designing the aircraft maximum attention was paid to completion of combat missions.

The He 111 B did not arouse Soviet interest in 1938. The hostilities in Spain opened the eyes of Soviet officialdom to the inferiority of the nation's aviation industry. There was nothing to match the modern German fighter aircraft. The first appearance of the Bf 109 shook the established reputation of the I-15 and I-16 fighters.

The Spanish Civil War also gave the *Luftwaffe* the opportunity to test its equipment and tactics under combat conditions. This allowed the Germans to pinpoint strengths and weaknesses, which led to improvements in aircraft design.

The Soviet industry proved less flexible. The I-15 and I-16 fighters used in Spain and the SB-2 bomber were all at the end of their development lives. But the Spanish Civil War did provide the impetus to accelerate the expansion of the Soviet air force. This was to prove especially important, as Germany and the USSR grew more confrontational. But then in 1939 the relationship between the two countries changed abruptly.

Development of the Dornier Falke was followed with interest. The photo above depicts serial number 3120, which was built in Dornier's Italian factory in Marino die Pisa. They type was of all-metal construction, and clearly followed the concepts incorporated in the Merkur transport. The aircraft was powered by a Hispano engine.

A second Dornier Falke that appears in Soviet aviation history was built by the Wright Aeronautical Corporation in the USA. The aircraft was powered by a Wright engine and differed from the earlier aircraft in having a modified radiator and new propeller. Note the minimal propeller clearance in flight attitude. It is not certain whether the machine was in fact delivered to the USSR. These photographs probably came from the manufacturer and were taken for demonstration purposes.

Right: The Spatz, an early Dornier design for a flying boat.

Center: The Soviet designer and historian V.B. Shavrov believes that two Heinkel He 5e floatplanes were purchased by the Soviet government and used by the flying school at Yeisk.

The ARK-Z-1 was developed by designer A.I. Zlokazov and was built in an airline maintenance facility in Irkutsk. The design was a slightly-modified PS-4 capable of carrying ten passengers.

These two photographs depict one of two Heinkel HD 37s tested by the flight test center in Moscow.

The Polikarpov I-7 was a copy of the Heinkel HD 37. The machine illustrated here is a prototype under test in Moscow.

Operational version of the Polikarpov I-7 in service with a Soviet air unit. The antenna suggests the installation of radio equipment.

Above: Detail shot of the tail section of a Polikarpov I-7.

Center: Winter version of the I-7 equipped with skis.

Below: This front view of the I-7 shows clearly the arrangement of the wing struts.

The Antonov TB-3 was a Soviet design created by the young designer A.N. Tupolev, however, its general concept owed a great deal to the designs of Junkers. Note the corrugated metal wings. By Soviet standards the all-metal aircraft was an extremely advanced design.

The reconnaissance version of the TB-3, the R-3 was a modification of the Tupolev design described above. The Junkers influence is very obvious.

Two Heinkel He 51 A fighter aircraft reached the Soviet Union after being captured by the Republicans in the Spanish Civil War. The machines were extensively tested by the NII VVS test center in the late 1930s. The Soviets found the design to be obsolete.

The capture of a Messerschmitt Bf 109 B by the Republicans proved a great stroke of luck for Soviet aviation. French test pilot Konstantin Rozanoff carried out initial trials in Spain, where this photograph was taken.

Konstantin Rozanoff in the cockpit of the Messerschmitt Bf 109 B-1 during flight trials in Spain. The aircraft has received the red wingtips carried by Republican aircraft.

Close-up of the cockpit area of the Bf 109 B-1.

The following series of photographs was taken at the NII VVS test center in the Soviet Union and was used to depict technical details of the Messerschmitt Bf 109 B-1. These photos illustrate details of early Bf 109 variants, and are thus something of a rarity. Note the English-style "spade grip" on the control column.

This photograph illustrates the arrangement of the lower engine access panels and the welded steel tube motor mounts. On later versions of the Messerschmitt fighter the motor mounts were castings.

Detail shot of the nose section and radiator housing. This early Bf 109 was equipped with a fixed-pitch wooden propeller. This was later replaced with a variable-pitch propeller.

Although the type was originally designed for three MG 17 machine-guns, this aircraft had just two, installed above the Jumo 210 D engine. The third weapon, which was supposed to fire through the propeller hub, was not installed. With 635 available horsepower, the Bf 109 B was certainly not overpowered.

Overall view of the Bf 109 B-1 at the NII VVS test center.

Another machine transferred from Spain was this example of the He 111 B. It, too, was captured by Republican forces. Note the red fuselage band, rudder, and wingtip markings. The rest of the aircraft's original finish, including markings, was retained.

The test center also produced detailed technical photos of the He 111 B, which today reside in Soviet archives. Here a photo of the bomb aimer's position in the nose of the aircraft.

View from the cockpit looking aft into the fuselage. To the right and left of the passageway to the rear fuselage are the bomb magazines.

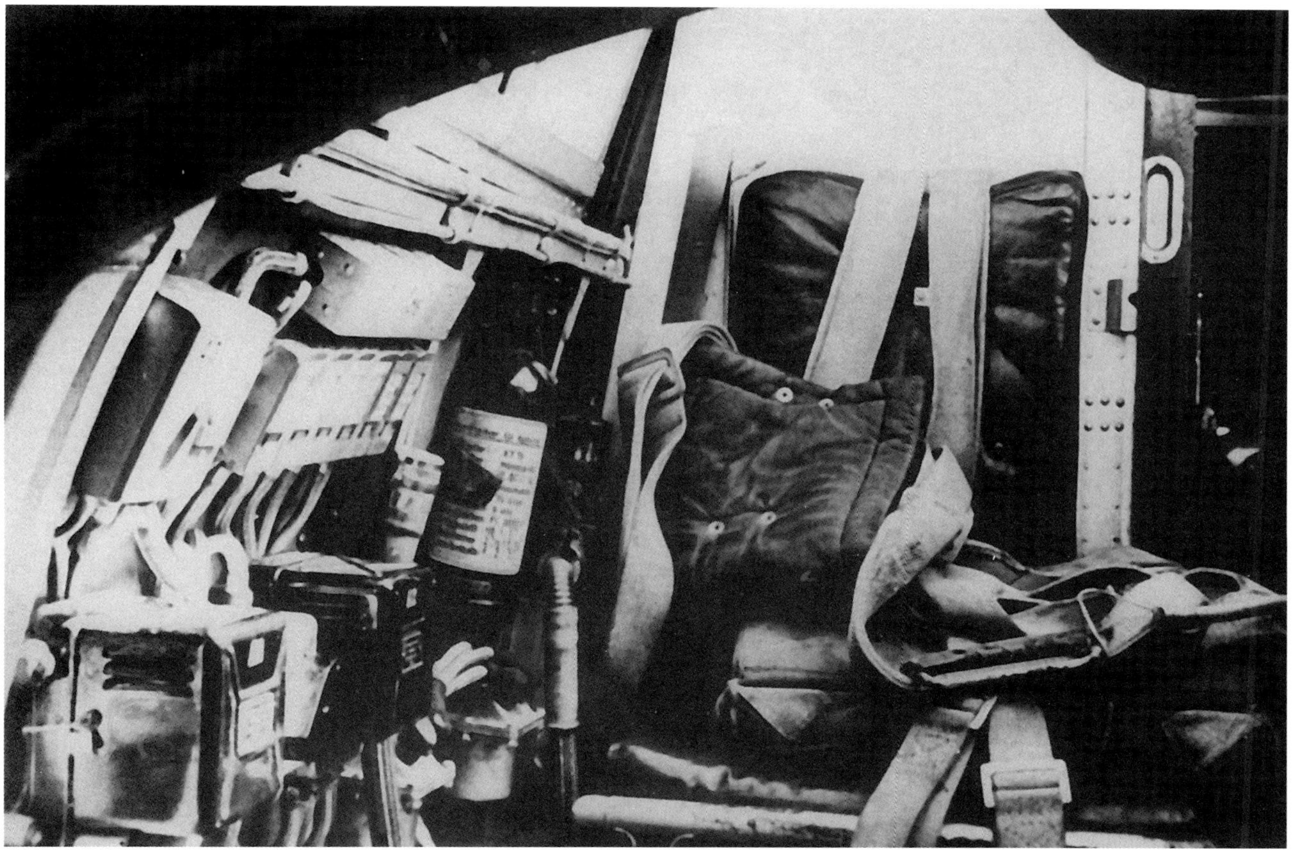

The radio operator's position.

The starboard engine.

Close-up of the DB 600 A engine.

The Heinkel He 111 B bearing the code 25-32 at the NII VVS test center airfield in Moscow.

A rare photograph of the He 111 B in flight during a test flight at the NII VVS test center.

Illustrated here is the Heinkel KR-1, a shipboard aircraft designed to operate from a catapult developed by Heinkel. The two photos at the top of the page depict the aircraft equipped with skis for winter operations. The aircraft with the number "5" on its rudder is equipped with twin machine-guns in the dorsal gun position.

The Heinkel KR-5 flown by well-known Arctic pilot Farikh is hauled on shore.

Heinkel KR-1 with the number "1" on its rudder is towed from a harbor.

Towing a Heinkel KR-1 with the identity number "2."

The following sequence of photographs illustrates a Heinkel KR-1 serving on the cruiser *Parijskaya Kommuna*. After landing, the aircraft was towed to the ship by a recovery boat, attached to the crane, and hoisted aboard.

The Heinkel KR-1 in position on the cruiser.

Tarpaulins were used to cover the cockpit and engine.

The next morning the aircraft was prepared for flight once again.

The flying boat in takeoff position on the catapult.

Start!!

1939-1941

German diplomatic successes in Austria and Czechoslovakia backed up by military power, and the events in Spain, showed that war was a definite possibility. The next victim was Poland, with Moscow, Berlin, London, and Paris all pursuing their own interests. From this confused situation emerged an unlikely friendship pact between Germany and the Soviet Union, known as the Molotov-Ribbentrop Pact. The agreement also included provisions for mutual technical support.

The pact also contained secret protocols for the division of Poland between the two powers. German diplomacy had overrun the Soviets, whose diplomats was much less experienced. In 1939 German and Soviet divisions met in Poland. In some cities there were even joint victory parades. The former enemies in Spain had become allies. Articles critical of Hitler disappeared from the front pages of Russian newspapers, replaced by features lauding German-Soviet cooperation.

Russian experiences in the Winter War against Finland convinced the authorities that the air force was in need of improvement. Once again the Russians turned to German armaments technology. The German-Soviet pact had made it possible to examine and even purchase German aircraft.

In March 1940 a Soviet delegation led by I.F. Tevosyan visited Germany. Representing the NII VVS test center were I.F. Petrov, head of the aviation department, and test pilot S.P. Suprun. Thirty-six aircraft of 12 different types were selected for purchase:

6 He 100	2 Do 215 B
5 Bf 109 E	3 Bü 131
5 Bf 110 C	3 Bü 133
2 Bf 108	2 Fi 156
1 Bf 209	3 Fw 58
2 Ju 88 A	2 Fa 266

The purchased machines began arriving in Moscow in early summer 1940, where they were assembled and then flown to the various test centers. Misunderstandings arose from the assembly of the first Bf 109. I.G. Rabkin, a young NII VVS engineer, and I.V. Julev, a technician, opened the crates and assembled the aircraft without the presence of German technicians.

Messerschmitt subsequently refused to guarantee the aircraft, however, no problems arose, and it was flown successfully. The remaining Bf 109s were assembled under the supervision of German technicians. Trials with the aircraft confirmed its excellent performance, which did not exactly thrill the Soviet military. The technological gap that had been revealed during operations in Spain had obviously widened tremendously.

The Bf 109 E-3 and Bf 110 C-4 fighters achieved speeds of 546 km/h (at a height of 5,000 meters) and 525 km/h (at 4,600 meters), more than 100 km/h faster than the most modern Soviet types, the I-15 and I-16. The German fighters also carried a significantly heavier armament. Weight of fire for the Bf 109 E was 2.49 kg/sec, and for the Bf 110 2.85 kg/sec.

Another type which attracted much attention was the He 100. The Soviets purchased the V1, V2, V4, V5, V6, and V7 prototypes. Although the Heinkel fighter possessed an excellent performance, it was ill-suited as a combat aircraft. The type's surface cooling system would have made it extremely vulnerable to enemy fire, while its armament of two 7.92-mm machine-guns was much too light.

More interesting results were achieved with the Ju 88 A and Do 215 B bombers. Their most impressive features were the ability to fly on one engine (in spite of all-metal construction), outstanding communications and navigation equipment, and the concentration of the crew in a small area, which eased crew coordination.

The Ju 88 was equipped with automatic dive brakes and self-sealing tanks, which increased its chances of survival greatly. Fuel tanks and lines were located in protected areas.

The Ju 88 took 18 minutes to reach 5,000 meters, while the Do 215, which had a somewhat lower takeoff weight, required just 10.8 minutes. The NII VVS praised the stability of all the aircraft it tested, with the exception of the He 100.

The prewar Soviet doctrine only allowed for stable bombers, while fighters were to have neutral stability. It was believed that this would endow them with superior maneuverability, however, trials with the German machines revealed this to be false.

The head of the investigating commission, A.I. Filin, said: "The current belief, that the best aircraft must be more difficult to fly, is absolutely false."

The Soviet trials gave a deep insight into the state of the German aviation industry. The layout of the all-metal designs displayed a high degree of robustness and special attention to crew comfort. A designated test pilot was assigned to each type. The following names are known:

Bf 109	I.D. Seliezniov
He 100	P.M. Popelniushenko
Do 215	P.F. Mushtaev

When the main program was over, other pilots flew the aircraft in order to build up a more subjective body of information. All of the pilots were impressed by the performances of the German aircraft and their equipment. The famous test pilot M.L. Gallay wrote in his memoirs:

The German aircraft had something which one could normally learn only through combat experience: simplicity, ease of operation for average pilots, unsurpassed reliability. They were proper soldier-aircraft.

Bf 109s, Bf 108s, Bü 131s, Fw 58s, and Fi 156s were purchased for closer examination.

One of these aircraft became very well known in the USSR. Following extensive testing, it was decided to produce a copy of the Fi 156 Storch with minor modifications. O.K. Antonov, who later became a famous designer, was placed in charge of the project.

Initially the aircraft was designated as an air ambulance. The first prototype, powered by a Renault 6Q engine, was completed in 1940. The general layout resembled that of the Fi 156, however, the Soviet aircraft was 47 kg heavier and payload was improved by 40 kg.

Takeoff and landing characteristics were identical to those of the Fi 156, however, the outbreak of war prevented large-scale production of the Soviet version, which was designated the OKA-38.

The Soviet aviation industry continued researching the purchased machines, but there was uncertainty as to German motives for delivering these modern aircraft. The prevailing opinion was that Germany wished to shock the Soviet specialists with the state of German technology. This was probably true in part, but nonetheless the German designs influenced the Soviet aviation industry and showed the way for future developments.

Shortly before the outbreak of war the Germans conducted a number of reconnaissance missions over the Soviet Union. The activities of *Aufklärungsgruppe Rowehl* broke new ground for both nations. The Rowehl unit was deployed as follows:

1. Staffel in Seerappen	area of operations Belorussia
2. Staffel in Insterburg	area of operations the Baltic States
3. Staffel in Bucharest	area of operations the Black Sea Coast

Two tactics were employed. One was flight at high altitude to evade Russian air defenses. On 20 June 1940 an aircraft on such a mission developed engine trouble and was forced to land near Minsk. The second method involved the use of civilian transport and communications aircraft.

Some aircraft landed at Soviet airfields, sometimes voluntarily, and sometimes forced down by Soviet fighters. It should be noted that the military districts involved were under the strict control of the central command, with orders to avoid any provocations.

The Soviet leadership was still convinced that Germany would not attack the USSR in 1941, and this belief allowed the reconnaissance flights to operate unmolested.

Emergency landings at Soviet airfields did not bring expected consequences. Aircraft and crews were quickly returned to Germany. The reasons offered for the border violations were almost always "loss of orientation" or "equipment failure."

Eighty violations of the border were reported between 27 March and 18 April 1941. On 15 April the Soviets discovered a torn map of the western USSR in an aircraft that landed near Rovno.

On 22 April the USSR filed an official protest against continued reconnaissance flights over the Soviet Union, however, the same diplomatic note remarked that no defensive measures were planned against these incursions.

From October 1939 until June 1941 approximately 500 German aircraft penetrated Soviet airspace, 150 in the six months preceding the German attack.

The Soviet Union purchased three examples of the Focke Wulf Fw 58 C-1 Weihe. The machine illustrated here is the second delivered, *Werknummer* 2537, registration D-OXWC. The German registration was retained during delivery.

The same machine following its arrival in Moscow.

This front view reveals the type's distinctive lines.

One of the Fw 58 Weihe purchased by the Soviets was a B-2. Its registration was D-OXWR (W.Nr. 2254). This photo was taken shortly after its arrival at the NII VVS test center.

The photos above illustrate the Focke Wulf Fw 58 B-2 from various angles.

Another aircraft purchased by the Soviets for test purposes was the Messerschmitt Bf 110 C-4. *Werknummer* 3130 is seen here. The aircraft wears Soviet markings. Note the code X-O beneath the port wing.

Two photographs of the same machine from different angles.

Close-up of the Bf 110 C-4's nose-mounted machine-guns.

Photograph of the cockpit area of the Bf 110 C-4.

Front and rear views reveal the clean lines of the Bf 110.

Three photographs of one of the two Dornier Do 215 B reconnaissance bombers purchased by the Soviet Union. These were taken at the NII VVS test center.

Excellent photograph of the cockpit of the Dornier Do 215 B-3 showing the instrumentation used during flight trials in Moscow. Note the machine-gun mount on the instrument panel.

Close-up of the dorsal gun position.

Ventral gun position on the underside of the Dornier Do 215 B-3.

Right main undercarriage element of the Do 215 B-3.

This Junkers Ju 88 was also purchased by the Soviet Union and extensively tested. Here it is seen still wearing its German civil registration D-AXVM.

Photo of the port engine nacelle, taken at the NII VVS test center.

In 1939 the Soviets purchased six examples of the He 100 fighter. These are some of the clearest photographs of the type ever published, and they illustrate well its clean lines.

This view from above reveals the integral wing-mounted radiators. While this arrangement offered reduced drag, the system was too vulnerable to damage for a combat aircraft. The basic design also proved too small to carry a worthwhile armament. Nevertheless, it may be assumed that the Heinkel fighter's aerodynamic layout influenced a number of Soviet designs.

Above: Front view of the Heinkel He 100.

The Heinkel He 100 found a place of honor in the TsAGI's technical study collection. Next to it is a Bf 109 G of JG 53 "Pik-As."

Five Messerschmitt Bf 109 E fighter aircraft were purchased by the Soviet Union in 1939 and tested extensively. Here a close-up of the aircraft's engine, in this case serial number 6376.

According to official sources this Fieseler Fi 156 Storch was delivered to the Soviet Union in 1940. Unfortunately, the aircraft's civil registration cannot be made out. The design of the Storch influenced that of the Soviet Antonov OKA-38.

The Fieseler Fi 156 Storch impressed the Soviets so much that a requirement was issued to the aviation industry for a similar aircraft. Designer O.K. Antonov conceived an aircraft whose design was based on the Fi 156. These three photographs depict the Antonov OKA-38, whose relationship to the Storch is undeniable.